THE PARABLES OF THE
KINGDOM

THE PARABLES OF THE
KINGDOM

By:

FR KYRILLOS FARAG

ST SHENOUDA PRESS
SYDNEY, AUSTRALIA
2024

The Parables of the Kingdom
By: Fr Kyrillos Farag

COPYRIGHT ©2024
St. Shenouda Press

All rights reserved. Except for brief quotations in critical publications or reviews, no part of this book may be reproduced in any manner without prior written permission from the publisher.

ST SHENOUDA PRESS
8419 Putty Rd,
Putty, NSW, 2330
Sydney, Australia

www.stshenoudapress.com

ISBN 13: 978-1-7635450-5-2

All scripture quotations, unless otherwise indicated, are taken from the New King James Version. Copyright © 1982 by Thomas Nelson, Inc. Used by permission. All rights reserved.

Table of Contents

The Parable of the Lamp and the Lampstand 11

The Parable of the Speck and the Plank 17

The Parable of the Lamp and the Lampstand 23

The Parable of a House Divided 31

The Parable of the Sower and the Seed 38

The Parable of the Wheat and the Tares 43

The Parable of the Mustard Seed 50

The Parable of the Leaven 57

The Parable of the Pearl 64

The Parable of the Net 70

The Parable of the Heart - Part 1 75

The Parable of the Heart - Part 2 80

The Parable of the Lost Sheep 88

The Parable of the Slave and Forgiveness 94

The Parable of the Eleventh Hour 102

The Parable of the Two Sons 108

The Parable of the Wicked Vinedressers 114

The Parable of the Wedding Feast - Part 1 117

The Parable of the Wedding Feast - Part 2 122

The Parable of the Fig Tree - Part 1 127

The Parable of the Wise, Faithful and Honest Steward.....133

The Parable of the Ten Virgins 137

The Parable of the Talents 144

The Parable of the Good Samaritan 151

The Parable of the Friend at Midnight.............................157

The Parable of the Foolish Rich Man................................161

The Parable of the Unjust Steward 164

The Parable of the Fig Tree - Part 2 167

The Parable of the Lost Coin 171

The Parable of the Lost Son 175

Preface

In the timeless tapestry of human history, few voices have resonated as profoundly and enduringly as that of Our Lord Jesus Christ. His teachings, conveyed through parables, continue to captivate hearts and minds across cultures and generations. Within the vast treasury of His parables, one recurring theme stands out like a radiant thread woven through the pages of the New Testament—a theme that unveils the very essence of His message: The Kingdom of God.

In this book, we embark on a profound journey, a simple one into the heart of our Lord Jesus Christ's parables, seeking not only to understand the eloquent stories He told, but also to grasp the profound truths they conceal. We invite you to join us on a pilgrimage into the Kingdom of God, a realm that Our Lord Jesus so masterfully illustrated through the vivid imagery of His parables.

According to **the Orthodox Study Bible, parables** are stories in word-pictures, revealing spiritual truth. The Hebrew and Aramaic words for *parable* also mean "allegory," "riddle," or "proverb." The Scriptures, especially the Gospels, are filled with parables - images drawn from daily life in the world to represent and communicate the deep things of God. *Parables give us glimpses of Him whose thoughts are not our thoughts and whose ways are not our ways* (Isaiah 55:8, 9). The truth communicated by Jesus' parables, however, is not evident to all who hear them. *The listener must have spiritual ears to hear,* and even then, not all have the same degree of understanding.

Thus, Jesus' statement that *"to those who are outside, all things come in parables"* (Mark 4:11) may be translated, *"... all things come in riddles."* Jesus' quotation of Isaiah 6:9, 10

(Matthew 13:14, 15) does not mean He used parables to blind the people or to lead them to punishment. On the contrary, it demonstrates that the people responsible for their own lack of receptivity: having grown dull and insensitive, they are unwilling to accept the message of the parables. As the mission of Isaiah in the Old Testament was to open the eyes of Israel to see the acts of God, so the parables of Jesus are intended to open the eyes of His hearers to the truth and lead them to produce the fruit of righteousness.

Parables challenge the hearer and call for faith to perceive the mysteries of the Kingdom. Insight into God's Kingdom does not come simply through an intellectual understanding of parables. Spiritual enlightenment is essentially a communication of faith in the Person, words, and deed of the Lord Jesus Christ. The use of parables was known in Jewish culture long before Jesus (2 Kings 12:1-4; Isiah 5:1-7). Jesus, however, brought the art of parables to perfection, relating aspects of the Kingdom and speaking of God Himself through vivid stories. His purpose was not only to reveal truth to those with hearts prepared. He wished to draw responsive hearts past the entrance and into the very reality of God's Kingdom which He proclaimed and inaugurated.

Among the familiar parables read on Sundays throughout the church Coptic year, those of the Sower (Luke 8:5-15); the Good Samaritan (Luke 10:25-37); the Rich Man and His Crops (Luke 12:16-21); the Great Supper (Luke 14:16-24); the Talents (Matthew 25:14-30); the Pharisee and the Tax Collector (Luke 18:10-14; and the Prodigal Son (Luke 15:11-32).

In opening to us the door of the Kingdom of heaven, the parables help us to love God and to know Him, to understand and believe His grace, mercy, and forgiveness, and to order our lives according to His Holy Word.

The parables of Our Lord Jesus are more than simple tales; they are windows into a reality that transcends the mundane. They invite us to see the world differently, to glimpse the hidden mysteries of the divine, and to participate in unfolding how we can inherit God's Kingdom. The Kingdom of God, as Our Lord Jesus envisioned it, is not an earthly empire with geographical boundaries; it is a spiritual reality, a reign of divine love, justice, and grace that permeates every aspect of our lives and world. The exploration of each parable serves as a pilgrimage into the Kingdom of God, a realm defined by divine love, justice, and grace. The book positions the parables as treasures filled with wisdom and insight, ready to be discovered by those who engage with them. It promises to unravel the layers of meaning and relevance in the context of contemporary life.

In the pages that follow, we will explore the depths of these parables, seeking to unearth their layers of meaning and relevance in the context of our lives today. Each parable serves as a treasure chest, filled with gems of wisdom and insight, waiting to be discovered by those who dare to open it.

As we delve into these parables, we will encounter the prodigal son seeking forgiveness, the Good Samaritan extending compassion, the mustard seed growing into a mighty tree, and many more timeless stories. Together, they will guide us to a richer understanding of the Kingdom of God, prompting us to contemplate our role in its realization in our lives and in the world.

This book is an exploration, an invitation, and a journey—a journey into the parables of Our Lord Jesus that leads us closer to the heart of the Kingdom of God. It is our hope that by the time you turn the last page, you will not only have a deeper understanding of these parables but also a renewed sense of purpose and a desire to actively participate in the ongoing story of God's Kingdom.

So, let us begin this expedition into the enchanting world of Our Lord Jesus' parables, with the Kingdom of God as our guiding star, illuminating our path and beckoning us to a richer, more profound experience of faith, love, and life. As we journey through these parables, let us reflect on the profound and eternal truth they convey—the Kingdom of God is not a distant realm but a reality that can be realized here and now. It is a kingdom of grace, love, justice, and compassion, waiting for us to recognize and embrace its presence in our daily lives.

May this book enrich, inspire, challenge, and ignite your imagination as we journey together through the parables of Our Lord Jesus, discovering the Kingdom of God in new and wondrous ways.

Acknowledgments

I extend my heartfelt gratitude to several remarkable blessed Fathers and selfless sisters and brothers whose unwavering dedication and invaluable contributions have played a pivotal role in the creation of this book.

A very warm thank you to my very reverend Father Marcus Tawfik for accepting to introduce this simple work and for always humbly guiding me with great wisdom and discernment during the journey of my life.

Blessed Sister Mervat Attia: Your tireless commitment to transcribing the original material for this project has been nothing short of extraordinary. Your diligence and perseverance have ensured that the essence of the content remains intact and accessible. Your selfless effort is deeply appreciated.

Blessed Tasony Mervat Attia: Your meticulous editing skills have been instrumental in refining the manuscript. Your keen eye for detail and commitment to excellence has significantly improved the overall quality of this work. I am grateful for your dedication to making this book the best it can be.

My blessed brother and son Jacob Wahib: Your tremendous effort in reviewing and editing the final copy of this book has been invaluable. Your insights and suggestions have contributed greatly to its clarity and coherence. Your commitment to perfection has not gone unnoticed, and I am thankful for your exceptional work.

My very Reverend Father Rafael Iskander, Father Matthew Attia and Father Michael Tanious: Your continuous support and encouragement have been a source of strength and inspiration throughout this endeavour. Your unwavering belief in the importance of this project has fuelled my determination to bring it to fruition. Your wisdom and guidance have been truly invaluable.

To all those who have offered their support and encouragement along this journey, your belief in the importance of this project has been a constant source of motivation. I extend my warmest thanks to my family, friends, and all who have played a role in bringing this work to fruition.

And finally, to the readers who embark on this voyage through the pages of this book, your interest and engagement are what make the endeavour of writing truly meaningful. Thank you for your curiosity and for joining me in exploring the subject matter of this book.

Introduction

Education through proverbs and real-life examples is one of the most effective teaching methods, bringing knowledge closer to the minds and hearts of individuals.

Our Lord and Saviour Jesus Christ exemplified this approach by enlightening people across generations. He taught the crowds through parables that resonated with their intellect, emotions, and memories. For instance, envision Jesus teaching the parable of the sower while standing among the people. Observing a farmer sowing seeds, He seized the opportunity to impart wisdom, declaring, *"A sower went out to sow his seed,"* as recorded in the Gospel of Saint Luke, chapter 8, verse 5. This is but one illustration of how Jesus utilized nature to convey spiritual truths, such as the creation of the universe by the Creator and the breath of life bestowed upon humanity by God.

Both creation and the human spirit are magnificent works of the Creator, revealed through His word and power. Throughout His teachings, Jesus consistently employed parables and metaphors. As stated in the Psalms and the Gospel of Saint Matthew, He fulfilled the prophecy: *"I will open My mouth in parables; I will utter things kept secret from the foundation of the world"* (Matthew 13:35).

It was no coincidence that Jesus used parables in His teaching. His method was foretold, and His disciples often inquired why He spoke in such a manner. His responses were invariably wise and aimed at fulfilling a specific purpose.

Dear readers, I invite you to explore the words inspired by the Holy Spirit, as presented through Father Kyrillos Farag.

May the Lord, in His boundless love, reward his efforts and enable us to use these teachings as preparation for His eternal kingdom. May every word heard, read, or experienced through various means be infused with the transformative power of the Holy Spirit. To Him be eternal glory. Amen.

Reverend Father Marcus Tawfik

Saint George Coptic Orthodox Church

Sydney, Australia

Chapter 1

The Parable of the Lamp and the Lampstand

The Radiant Call: Unveiling the Wisdom of Christ's Parables

Let us delve into the wisdom of our Lord Jesus Christ through his parables. These stories hold profound truths about our faith and spiritual teachings, and we can gain valuable insights by applying them to our lives in this world that gradually undergoes calving from the word of God and Christianity.

Instead of solely engaging in meditation and contemplation of these parables, it is essential to complement these practices with earnest prayers, imploring that their profound messages permeate our lives in a subtle, invisible, and mystical manner, thereby exerting a positive influence on those in our midst. We firmly hold the conviction that the "word of God is living and powerful, sharper than any two-edged sword, penetrating to the very core of soul and spirit, joints and marrow, discerning the thoughts and intentions of the heart" (Hebrews 4:12). This divine message operates mystically, wielding its own inherent power and grace, intricately embedded and stored within.

One of the most well-known parables spoken by our Lord Jesus is found in the Gospel of Saint Matthew chapter 5:14-16. During His Sermon on the Mount, our Lord Christ imparted these famous words: *"You are the light of the world. A city on a hill cannot be hidden. Nor do people light a lamp and put it under a basket, but on a lampstand, and it gives light to all in the house. Let your light shine before others, that they may see your good deeds and glorify your Father in heaven."*

Four terms are used to illustrate the Christian character

Four terms are used to illustrate the Christian character: salt, light, lamp, and lampstand. Salt was used by the Jewish people to sprinkle on oil to give brightness to the lamps. Salt also was used to purify and preserve food. Jesus Christ used these illustrations to show the function of the Christian character, to give brightness to life and to preserve society from the forces of decay. The lamp and lampstand were used as an illustration for everyday life of the Jewish people. The significance is that the Disciples of our Lord Jesus Christ and all Christians are obliged to present the light of the Gospel to the world. Jesus named Himself the Light to illuminate the Apostles and disciples as they present the Light of the Gospel to the world, shining before man to show God's good works and to guide man in glorifying the True God.

You are the salt of the earth and the light of the world, an influence achieved not merely through words or deeds but by the power of presence. Salt affects its surroundings simply by being true to its nature, requiring neither speech nor action. In the Gospel of Saint Luke, Jesus cautions that if salt loses its flavor, it becomes useless—not suitable even for the soil or the compost heap. This reflects the historical use of salt, particularly that harvested from the Dead Sea, which contained a mix of sodium chloride, potassium chloride, and other minerals.

The Parable of the Lamp and the Lampstand

In agriculture, plants require balanced nutrients: phosphate for strong roots, nitrates for leafy growth, and potash for flowers and fruit. The salt from the Dead Sea was prized as a fertilizer due to its potassium content, which nurtured beneficial plants while inhibiting harmful ones. This dual role serves as a profound metaphor: Christians are called to be the 'salt of the soil,' cultivating what is good and curbing what is harmful. The message is clear—Christians should stand out, quietly yet powerfully shaping their environment.

However, salt can only make an impact if present in sufficient quantity; a light sprinkling is inadequate. Unfortunately, there is too little 'salt' in society today, contributing to moral and social decay. Efforts such as lobbying or protesting may achieve minor victories, but without a substantial and committed Christian presence, meaningful change remains difficult. True transformation occurs not through what this minority says or does, but simply through their presence and influence. Yet, living as a Christian grows increasingly challenging as societal values drift further from faith. We need more 'salt'— Christians deeply engaged in their communities, illuminating and preserving what is good in a world that urgently needs it."

When we think about the phrase "you are the light" we can relate it to how the sun's light is ever-present when we are awake. Similarly, God tells us that we are to be a source of light for those around us. Whether at work, school, university, commuting, shopping etc. or in any aspect of our lives, our aim is to shine as a beacon of light in a world plagued by sin, hatred, selfishness, and negativity. It is the Holy Spirit residing within us that enlightens us, not through mere words but through living a genuine and sincere life.

Every prayer, every word we read in the Bible, and every commandment we obey serve to make us a beacon of light. While we may not perceive this light within ourselves, those around us will undoubtedly see its radiance and recognize that we are different. Just as light follows a straight path, Christians are encouraged to lead their lives in a manner that is upright and straightforward. *"For as that lamp enlightens the house, so do ye light up the souls of men; and as this is useless when concealed, so is it with you too."* (Chrysostom, Homilies on Matthew)

Bishop Epiphanius a radiant light in our generation

Allow me to share the inspiring story of a truly enlightened individual from our generation:

The late **Bishop Epiphanius** (1954–2018), Abbot of the Monastery of Saint Macarius was one of the most beloved and widely-respected Coptic scholars of the 21st century. Originally a doctor from Tanta, Tadros Zaki Tadros became a monk of the Monastery of Saint Macarius in 1984 at the age of 29, taking the name Epiphanius al-Makary. As a former doctor, he provided medical care to ill and elderly monks at the monastery, often accompanying them on trips abroad to receive treatment and providing palliative care. His keen intellect and eye for detail caused him to be singled out by the monastery's famous Abbot, to work in the monastery's library. At Fr Matthew's command, he was ordained a priest in 2002 (despite his protestations). In 2013, he was elected to succeed Fr Matthew (who had passed away in 2006) as Abbot of the monastery, and was ordained a bishop by HH Pope Tawadros II: a role he carried out with deep, often confronting, humility (e.g. sitting at the back of churches and lecture halls, and refusing to allow people to make the prostration customary for greeting a Coptic bishop, insisting: "If you prostrate before me, I will prostrate before you!"). Pope Tawadros drew heavily on Bishop Epiphanius' theological learning and his deep monastic experience, appointing him to many delegations and committees, attracting the ire of those who opposed the much-debated theological legacy of Fr Matta El Meskeen, He was tragically murdered in 2018.

The Parable of the Lamp and the Lampstand

I came across a book about his life, published by the Monastery of Saint Macarius shortly after his passing. The book was a compilation of memories shared by His Holiness Pope Tawadros II, fellow bishops, monks, and disciples from around the world who had the privilege of knowing him. Despite his abundant knowledge, Bishop Epiphanius remained remarkably humble and unpretentious. If you were to visit his monastery, you would never have guessed he was a bishop; he wore simple attire, sat on the floor instead of a chair, and engaged with his disciples, leaving a profound impact with his humility and boundless love for all.

Representing the Coptic Church at various conferences, including the one in Italy in 2015, he demonstrated not only extensive knowledge but also fluency in several languages, such as Latin, Greek, English, French, and, of course, Coptic and Arabic. When questioned about church schisms, he would humbly respond, "Forgive me, I am not a theologian. I do not understand divisions; I only understand the unity of the Church." Such words elicited three minutes of applause from those who listened.

He was often likened to a celestial visitor who graced our world for a brief time, yet his presence transformed the lives of many. During the events of 25 January 2011, a considerable number of prisoners escaped from a jail near the Monastery of Saint Macarius in Wadi El-Natroun "measure of hearts". Bishop Epiphanius welcomed them into his monastery and provided them with food, leaving a profound impact on everyone present.

His life story serves as a reminder that true enlightenment is not found in grandiose displays of knowledge but in the simplicity of a life lived in humility and love. He illuminated the lives of those around him, leaving an indelible mark.

Indeed, he serves as a remarkable model of a person living as a shining light in the world. This prompts us to ask ourselves: when we go to work, do we radiate that divine light to those around us? Can others see the light of God shining through us?

Or do we simply blend in with the crowd, indistinguishable from one another?

The ultimate purpose of letting one's light shine is to bring glory to God.

Saint Maximus the Confessor comments on the famous phrase from the gospels "no one lights a lamp and puts it under a bushel, but on a stand, and it gives light to all in the house" (Matthew 5:15 and Luke 8:16 and 11:33). To fail to progress from the letter of Scripture to its spirit is to allow the light of divine revelation to remain hidden as under a basket.

The ultimate purpose of letting one's light shine is to bring glory to God. When others see the good works and the light of faith in believers, they should be drawn to give glory to God, recognizing His presence and goodness. The message of the Gospel and the good works of believers should be evident to all, having a positive impact on those around them.

Contemplating your footprint in this world is a deep and introspective inquiry. It provides a chance for introspection about your distinct purpose, contributions, and the imprint you wish to leave during your journey on Earth. Bear in mind that, akin to your physical fingerprint, your unique mark on the world is exclusive to you, and it has the potential to transform as you evolve. It mirrors your individuality, encapsulating your experiences and the positive influence you wield in the world. Persist in your exploration, personal growth, and the mindful choices you make, ensuring they resonate with the lasting impact you aspire to create.

As we conclude this chapter, let us turn to prayer, seeking the guidance of the One who is the true Light that came into the world. Let us beseech Him: "You are the true light who came into the world to enlighten it. I am from the world but not of it. May Your Spirit within me grant me the ability to live as a light.

Chapter 2

The Parable of the Speck and the Plank

The Danger of Hypocrisy: Confronting Our Own Flaws Before Judging Others

This is one of the simpler parables, but it carries a significant impact on our spiritual journey. In Matthew 7:1-4, it is written, *"Judge not, that you be not judged. For with what judgment you judge, you will be judged; and with the measure you use, it will be measured back to you. And why do you look at the speck in your brother's eye, but do not consider the plank in your own eye? Or how can you say to your brother, 'Let me remove the speck from your eye;' and look, a plank is in your own eye? Hypocrite! First remove the plank from your own eye, and then you will see clearly to remove the speck from your brother's eye."*

Passing judgment on others is the most significant obstacle to maintaining a pure heart, as it diverts attention away from our own sins and directs it towards others' mistakes. While I might have many issues to work on internally, requiring effort and struggle to overcome, I find myself focusing on the weaknesses and deficiencies of others. To draw a parallel, it is like a person having a death in their own family but abandoning their relatives to mourn their neighbour's loss. This parable strongly condemns hypocrisy, where one pretends to be morally upright while harbouring significant moral or ethical issues. It reminds us that self-righteous judgment can often be a form of hypocrisy.

Our Lord commands us not to judge individuals. Why? Because only God can penetrate the depths of people's hearts, souls, and minds to understand their motives. It is not merely a matter of being morally upright; it is a task beyond our human capability and authority.

Why will we be judged with the same measure? Because our duty is to introspect, to assess ourselves honestly. Instead of scrutinizing others, we should focus on confronting our own sins and shortcomings. Aren't we prone to recognizing sins in others that afflict us as well?

Nevertheless, even when judging ourselves, we must exercise caution. Modern psychology attests to the complexity of our inner selves, with layers of thoughts and emotions that may elude our conscious awareness. Saint Paul seemed cognizant of this when he remarked, "I care very little if I am judged by you or by any human court; indeed, I do not even judge myself. My conscience is clear, but that does not make me innocent. It is the Lord who judges me." (1 Corinthians 4:1). Considering this wisdom, Father Tom Hopko wisely counselled us to *"Be merciful with yourself and with others"*.

The teachings of my confessor and spiritual guide, Father Bishoy Yassa, have left an indelible mark on my soul. His wise counsel echoes in my mind, especially during moments of spiritual reflection and self-examination. He often encouraged me to envision myself seated in the tender embrace of our Lord Jesus Christ, recounting my sins and weaknesses. In this sacred imagery, I feel the comforting presence of Christ's arms enveloping me, offering solace and acceptance. It is a profound and transformative experience, one that fosters genuine repentance and renewal.

This kind of judgment is truly disruptive. Saint Augustine the Great wisely observed, *"If your brother falls into the sin of anger and you judge him, you will fall into the sin of hatred by judging him."* There is a crucial distinction between anger and hatred. Saint Augustine also pointed out, *"The root of judgment is a lack of love; if there was love, and it would cover all flaws."* This is why many saints worked hard to shield weaker members who had fallen and surrounded them with support to rescue them. It is akin to casting a lifeline with a hook to catch onto and save that struggling person.

In this quote, Saint Augustine emphasizes the potential negative consequences of judging others, particularly when they have fallen into sin or made mistakes. He warns that when we pass judgment on someone, especially in the context of their failings or shortcomings, we can ourselves become ensnared by the sin of hatred. This observation underscores the idea that harsh and uncharitable judgment can lead to the erosion of our own virtues and moral character.

Saint Augustine's teachings align with broader Christian principles of forgiveness, empathy, and love for one's neighbour. His words encourage us believers to approach others with humility, recognizing their own imperfections and need for forgiveness, and to resist the temptation to condemn or harbor hatred.

Overall, this quote serves as a reminder of the importance of practicing mercy and understanding in our interactions with others, rather than rushing to judgment or condemnation. It underscores the idea that our response to others' shortcomings should be guided by love and a desire for their well-being, rather than by harsh judgment.

As we progress along the path of holiness, we draw closer to God with a pure heart. Our mouths and minds close, and the habit of judging others ceases.

Compassion Over Condemnation: Lessons from Christ, Saints, and Spiritual Leaders

Now, let me share a touching story about Pope Kyrillos VI, the great Saint of our modern time and the was the 116th Pope of Alexandria and Patriarch of the See of Saint Mark, who stood up for a servant struggling with alcohol addiction. When others hurried to inform the Pope of this servant's actions and expose and emphasize his sin, the Pope responded by calling him his blessed son. One day, these individuals followed the man to a bar, waiting until he was completely drunk. When he became unconscious, they wrapped him in a rug and brought him to the Pope, saying, "Here is your 'blessed son.'" How did the Pope react? Reflecting on Christ's teachings, he knelt down, removed the man's shoes, placed a pillow under his head, and covered him with a blanket. When these individuals who shamefully brought the man saw how the Pope reacted in great love and compassion on this poor man, they attempted to kneel and help Pope Kyrillos to take off the man's shoes. He told these people not to approach his son, the son they had stripped of dignity by exposing his weakness. When the man woke up in an unfamiliar place, the Pope embraced him and advised him to attend church and pray for me. The man was moved that from that moment on, the man led a life of purity and holiness. This story of Pope Kyrillos VI beautifully captures the essence of Christ-like compassion, humility, and the transformative power of unconditional love. When confronted with a servant's struggle, the Pope chose not to judge or condemn, but to extend grace, dignity, and mercy. This act of profound humility, kneeling to care for a man whom others sought to shame, reflects a deep understanding of the Gospel message: that every soul is precious and redeemable in the eyes of God.

Pope Kyrillos' response serves as a powerful reminder of how we, as followers of Christ, are called to treat others, especially those who are struggling. Instead of adding to the weight of guilt and shame, he offered acceptance, patience, and a path toward healing. His actions embodied the heart of Christ's teachings, demonstrating that real change often begins not with harsh words or judgment, but with acts of kindness and a willingness to meet people where they are.

The Pope's tender care for the man, even in his lowest moment, led to a transformation that no amount of rebuke could have achieved. It is a testament to the impact of love that sees beyond faults and failures, treating each person not as they are but as they could be. This story challenges us to rethink how we respond to the weaknesses of others, urging us to act with the same grace and mercy that Pope Kyrillos showed—transformative love that reaches into the depths of brokenness and lifts others up.

Saint John Chrysostom said, *"Correct your brother in private, commend him in public, and pray for him in secret."* This saying underscores the importance of approaching our brothers and sisters in faith with humility, love, and discretion, rather than passing harsh judgment. It encourages a spirit of correction guided by genuine care and a desire for their spiritual well-being.

Let us remember not to pass judgment on others, for we do not know their circumstances, emotions, life experiences, upbringing, or how they have been treated in their lives. The principle of reciprocity is present in this parable. Just as you judge others, you will be judged. It underscores the Golden Rule: "Do to others as you would have them do to you."

Saint Moses the Black timeless lesson

Saint Moses the Black lived during the fourth century in Egypt. Once a brother had been caught in a particular sin, and the abbot asked Saint Moses to come to the church and render judgment. He came reluctantly, carrying on his back a leaking bag of sand. When he arrived, the brothers asked him why he was carrying such a thing. He simply said, "This sand is my sins which are trailing out behind me, while I go to judge the sins of another." At that reply, the brothers forgave the offender and returned to focusing on their own salvation rather than the sins of their brother. He also proclaimed, "Fire and water are incompatible; similarly, condemning others doesn't align with those seeking repentance."

Saint John of the Ladder wisely said that when you condemn your brother, the blessing of the Holy Spirit will be cut off from you, and you will stumble over your brother. The wise Fathers warned that, over time, you will eventually fall into the same sin you judge in others.

The message from this parable is clear: Refrain from judgment; instead, put in the effort, seek, pray, and beseech the Lord not to highlight and judge the wrongdoings of others.

In essence, this parable calls us to exercise humility, empathy, and self-awareness in our interactions with others. It teaches us that our response to others' shortcomings should be guided by love, compassion, and a desire for their well-being, rather than by harsh judgment. As one of the righteous Fathers aptly put it, "It is not my concern; let me focus on only myself." This profound message challenges us to continually strive for spiritual growth and to cultivate a heart filled with love, respect and understanding for our fellow travellers on the path of faith. I would like to end this simple commentary on this parable with a remarkable and giant saying from an amazingly simple Mother Theresa who said, *"If you judge people, you have no time to love them."* think about how truthful and beautiful is this?

Chapter 3

The Parable of the Lamp and the Lampstand

New Life in Christ: Leaving the Old Behind and Relying on Divine Strength

This parable comes up in various gospel accounts. In Saint Matthew 9:15, it is written, *"And Our Lord Jesus said to them, 'Can the friends of the bridegroom mourn as long as the bridegroom is with them? But the days will come when the bridegroom will be taken away from them, and then they will fast No one puts a piece of unshrunk cloth on an old garment; for the patch pulls away from the garment, and the tear is made worse. Nor do they put new wine into old wineskins, or else the wineskins break, the wine is spilled, and the wineskins are ruined. But they put new wine into new wineskins, and both are preserved.'"*

The depth of this parable centres on the term '**new**', which is echoed throughout. The core message from the Lord Our Lord Jesus is that simply patching up does not work. Imagine launching a New Year, yet still carrying old baggage in our lives, I guess we all did this in our lives?

From the perspective of Our Lord Jesus' teachings, the concept of the "old man" and the "new man" frequently symbolizes the profound transformation experienced by a believer upon joining the body of Christ- the church after accepting Our Lord Jesus Christ as Lord and Saviour, typically realized through the sacrament of baptism. These terms are predominantly present in the New Testament, particularly in the writings of the Apostle Saint Paul.

- **Old Man:** The "old man" refers to a person's state before coming to faith in Our Lord Jesus Christ It represents the unregenerate or sinful nature that is characterized by disobedience to God, a focus on self, and a life separated from God due to sin. In this state, individuals are spiritually dead and under the dominion of sin.

- **New Man:** The "new man" represents the transformed state of a believer after accepting Our Lord Jesus Christ It signifies a spiritual rebirth or regeneration through faith in Our Lord Jesus. When a person becomes a Christian, they receive a new nature empowered by the Holy Spirit. This new nature is characterized by righteousness, holiness, and a desire to live in obedience to God.

Our Lord Jesus Christ wants us to grasp that He is all about providing everything anew – a new self, reborn through baptism and rose with Our Lord Jesus Christ our weakness lies in our inclination towards patches, opting for a cut-and-paste approach. We coexist with old ways while trying to fit them into a new life. Our Lord Jesus Christ is telling us that just does not work.

Christ likened the new life in Him to a fresh garment. Reflecting on our former life and attempting to preserve parts of it is akin to mending an old dress with a fragment from a new garment—a futile endeavour. The analogy Our Lord used implies that integrating elements of the new life with the old is impractical; it results in tearing, and the new piece does not align with the old (Luke 5:36). The Church emphasizes the necessity of fully abandoning the old life when initiating a new life with Jesus Christ, aligning with the biblical principle that old things have passed away (2 Corinthians 5:17).

Some individuals attempt to live dual lives, seeking to reconcile worldly pursuits with a connection to God. This echoes the Old Testament warning delivered by the prophet Elijah, questioning those who vacillate between two opinions—God and Baal *"And Elijah came to all the people, and said, "How long will you falter between two opinions? If the Lord is God, follow Him; but if Baal, follow him." But the people answered him not a word."* (1 Kings 18:21). A genuine new life in Christ involves the burial of the old self, a transformation symbolized by the Mystery of Baptism, where the old man is buried and resurrected with Christ (Colossians 2:12).

His Eminence Metropolitan Youssef, metropolitan of the Coptic Orthodox Diocese of the Southern United States teaches us that there are two main obstacles stare us in the face as we journey through the process of renewing our lives.

1. **Adhering to the old:** A new life with Christ entails a fresh start and when we are about to start a new life in Him, we should sever ourselves from all that can hinder the progress of that relationship. A prominent figure in the Holy Bible who had the courage to do that without regret or return is Saint Paul. According to worldly standards he was considered a successful prominent figure *"If anyone else thinks he may have confidence in the flesh, I more so: circumcised the eighth day, of the stock of Israel, of the tribe of Benjamin, a Hebrew of the Hebrews; concerning the law, a Pharisee; concerning zeal, persecuting the church; concerning the righteousness which is in the law, blameless"* (Philippians 3:4-6). However, after encountering Christ and giving his life over to His service Saint Paul came to realize that *"But what things*

were gain to me, these I have counted loss for Christ. Yet indeed I also count all things loss for the excellence of the knowledge of Christ Jesus my Lord, for whom I have suffered the loss of all things, and count them as rubbish, that I may gain Christ and be found in Him" (Philippians 3:7-9). He knew exactly that the two can never match nor blend together. Another example is Saint Mathew whom the church put as an example of relinquishing everything for the sake of Christ. A Levite, of noble, rich, influential prestigious descent who upon hearing the Lord Jesus Christs call follow me, he immediately arose and followed Him (Matthew 9:9). Adhering to the old could always be supported with fear of the unknown, uncertainty of the future and unwillingness to leave the Comfort Zone. Today Christ is calling you to leave behind your sinful life and come and follow him *today," if you will hear His voice do not harden your hearts* "(Hebrews 3:7-8). *"And now with all our heart we follow you; we fear you and seek your presence. Do not put us to shame"* (Daniel 3:41-42, Septuagint). That was the prayer of Azariah, one of the three young men.

2. **Reliance on one's efforts:** Many would want to live a new life in Christ. However, they do not know how. They think that they could do it themselves by increasing their efforts and promises, only soon to discover their failure and so fall into depression and lose hope. Such people need to know that no matter what they do and how they do it, change comes from God. His Holiness Pope Shenouda III has expressed this spiritual reality in a beautiful poem that says:

> With bitter tears I wetted my bed
> And with promises You I fed
> To Your love I will stick
> Like to a rock I will stick

The Parable of the Lamp and the Lampstand

And never to sin will I return
Severe war upon me came
And indeed, sinful I became
I cried from my heart
Id stop, and again Id start
And to sin I did return
Pridefully, my will I attempted to strengthen
In vain, my promises I intended to lengthen
With efforts and strivings heated
Myself I had cheated
And to sin I did return

I cried bitterly
I pleaded strongly
To no one else I will go
My weaknesses them I know
O Lord on me have mercy
No matter how much I fought
Not by my efforts as I thought
Power is from heaven above
And with Your Spirit, from above
To sin will I never return

Thus is the ultimate result of the efforts of whosoever relies on himself in building his spiritual life and renewing his promises. All the spiritual practices such as fasting, attending church, praying, reading the Word of God are all means to an end and not an end in them. All they do is they place us in the orbit of Gods mercy and allow it to find us and work in us. Change is impossible without God's Grace and Mercy.

Incompatibility of the Old and the New: Our Lord Jesus uses the metaphor of clothing and wine containers to illustrate that the old and the new are often incompatible. Trying to patch an old garment with unshrunk cloth or storing new wine in old wineskins will lead to negative outcomes. The old and the new cannot coexist harmoniously.

The Power of Spiritual Decisions: Embracing Transformation Through Choices

This parable carries a spiritual message. It emphasizes the need for a new and receptive heart to fully receive and embrace the teachings and message of Our Lord Jesus. It suggests that trying to fit new spiritual insights or truths into an old and rigid mindset may result in spiritual conflict or loss.

Consider the story of Zacchaeus in the gospel as written by Saint Luke chapter 19, who initiated his fresh start with an all-new approach. When Our Lord Jesus Christ reached out to him, Zacchaeus made a pivotal choice. This is the crux – a new life requires a resolute decision. Zacchaeus stood his ground and declared to Our Lord Jesus, *"Look, Lord, I give half of my goods to the poor; and if I have taken anything from anyone by false accusation, I restore fourfold"* (Luke 19:8).

Our life achievements are linked to the decisions we make; to work diligently is a decision. To love is also a decision. To relocate is a decision, to walk with Our Lord Jesus Our Lord Jesus Christ is a decision, praying is a decision, reading the Bible is a decision, forgiving, forgetting, and persevering are decisions, forsaking all and following Our Lord Jesus is a decision, and having courage and confessing is a decision.

There are some moments where we must make potentially life-changing decisions, and these critical junctures abound in life. Joseph's refusal to commit the sin when confronted by

Potiphar's wife; was a decision. Abraham's consent to heed God's call, even if it meant sacrificing his son Isaac was a decision. Saint Anthony selling all he had to follow our Lord Our Lord Jesus that was a decision. The disciples leaving behind their possessions to follow our Lord Our Lord Jesus that was a decision. Conversely, there were those who could not make spiritual decisions, like the rich young man who opted not to follow Our Lord Jesus. All these decisions where initiated and inspired by the grace of God. The grace of God often plays a subtle but powerful role in our decision-making process, especially in moments of significant choice. It might not always be immediately apparent

Are we proactive in our spiritual decisions?

What hampers our decision-making? Could it be that our love for Our Lord Jesus Christ is feeble in our hearts? Are our eyes and hearts ensnared by worldly matters? Are we still gripped by earthly desires and temptations, unable to break free? Does sin hold us captive, its grip connected to our senses and hearts, like a balloon anchored by a string?

I know of a young man who led a reckless, godless life, distant from God. Many attempted to steer him back to God without success. One night, the late Pope Shenouda III visited him in Australia in a vision and gently said, "My dear son, I'm disheartened by your life. Why not return and embrace a life with God? Attend church tomorrow, confess, and repent." This visit touched the young man, prompting him to make a firm decision to turn his life around. Today, he is grateful to the Lord and lives a vibrant, joyful life with God. Today, he is one of the most blessed and spirit led servants that I have met.

Zacchaeus' choice stemmed from his encounter with Our Lord Jesus Our Lord Jesus Christ, which transformed his life.

In summary, the Parable of the Old and the New Garments teaches the importance of being open to spiritual transformation, embracing the newness of Our Lord Jesus Christ's message, and recognizing that old and rigid religious practices may not be compatible with the Gospel. It invites believers to cultivate a heart and mindset that can receive and preserve the transformative power of the new wine of Our Lord Jesus' teachings.

Let us reflect and ask ourselves, have we encountered Our Lord Jesus? Have we seen Him, loved Him, felt His radiance, love, and joy within our hearts? Reflect on this and make a decision that will transform your life.

Chapter 4

The Parable of a House Divided

This parable is found in the Gospel of Saint Matthew (12:24-30)

"When the Pharisees heard it they said, "This fellow does not cast out demons except by Beelzebub, the ruler of the demons." But Our Lord Jesus knew their thoughts, and said to them: "Every kingdom divided against itself is brought to desolation, and every city or house divided against itself will not stand. If Satan casts out Satan, he is divided against himself. How then will his kingdom stand? And if I cast out demons by Beelzebub, by whom do your sons cast them out? Therefore they shall be your judges. But if I cast out demons by the Spirit of God, surely the kingdom of God has come upon you. Or how can one enter a strong man's house and plunder his goods, unless he first binds the strong man? And then he will plunder his house. He who is not with Me is against Me, and he who does not gather with Me scatters abroad."

The Parable of a House Divided, found in the New Testament in the Gospels of Saint Matthew, Saint Mark, and Saint Luke, is a teaching of our Lord Jesus in response to the accusation that He casts out demons by the power of Beelzebub, the prince of demons. While this specific parable does not have direct quotes from the early Church Fathers, we can provide a commentary from an Orthodox Christian perspective along with some relevant principles from early Christian thought.

In this parable, Our Lord Jesus addresses a profound affliction that can affect the body, akin to a medical condition known as autoimmune diseases. These illnesses manifest when the body's immune system mistakenly targets healthy cells, launching attacks on various organs. When God created the human body, He endowed it with a resilient immune system to combat pathogens and invaders. However, in certain circumstances, a malfunction occurs, leading the body to perceive its own cells as threats. Consequently, the body generates proteins that attack its own tissues, essentially turning against itself.

As Saint Cyprian quoted "God is one, and Christ is one, and His Church is one, and the faith is one, and the people are joined into a substantial unity of body by the cement of concord. Unity cannot be severed; nor can one body be separated by a division of its structure, nor torn into pieces, with its entrails wrenched asunder by laceration. Whatever has proceeded from the womb cannot live and breathe in its detached condition but loses the substance of health."

In this parable, Our Lord Jesus Christ is addressing a similar kind of strife: division among parents within their own homes and families, or conflicts among church servants leading to discord. Such divisions are destructive, for they leave only losers, no winners. This is why Our Lord Jesus Christ stated, "*A house divided against itself will not stand,*" leading to ruin, devastation, and loss. A house built over years can be destroyed in seconds. Our Lord Jesus Christ's final words in the Gospel of Saint John are, "*That they may all be one, as You, Father, are in Me, and I in You; that they also may be one in Us*" (John 17:21). Our Lord Jesus Christ came to unite all, and at the end of this parable, He remarked, *"He who is not with Me is against Me, and he who does not gather with Me scatters abroad."*

These divisions create fractures within families, marriages, and, consequently, lead to a divided Church. The existence of over 30,000 Christian denominations is a staggering number and a serious scandal, bringing shame to the entire Christian community.

Top of Form

The opposite of division is unity. If you have ever experienced division in your family or church, you know the bitterness and pain it carries and leaves behind. On the other side, unity is healing; fostering peace, empowerment, and growth. Unity carries God's will and radiates the fragrance of Our Lord Jesus Christ Saint Paul addressed unity among fellow believers in his Epistle to the Ephesians. *"I, therefore, the prisoner of the Lord, beseech you to walk worthy of the calling with which you were called, with all lowliness and gentleness, with longsuffering, bearing with one another in love, endeavouring to keep the unity of the Spirit in the bond of peace. There is one body and one Spirit, just as you were called in one hope of your calling; one Lord, one faith, one baptism; one God and Father of all, who is above all, and through all, and in you all."* (Ephesians 4:1-6)

If we inquire, "What fuels division?" We will find the major catalyst is the **ego**. It is our greatest adversary, the church's nemesis, and a foe to families. Our Lord Jesus Christ taught that this ego must perish, replaced by self-denial; the grain of wheat that must fall and die before yielding fruit (John 12:24). The triumphant Our Lord Jesus Christian faces down their ego and crucifies it: *"Those who belong to Our Lord Jesus Christ Our Lord Jesus have crucified the flesh with its passions and desires"* (Galatians 5:24).

Imagine if this ego ceased to exist, we would all follow one, Our Lord Jesus Christ Sects and religious divisions would vanish. When someone causes division, they often have a concealed agenda – some personal gain like a desire for a particular position, or any other ulterior motive. Our Lord Jesus grieved, saying, *"O Jerusalem, Jerusalem, the one who kills the prophets and stones those who are sent to her! How often I wanted to gather your children together, as a hen gathers her chicks under her wings, but you were not willing!"* (Matthew 23:37). Unity is our strength, especially as Our Lord Jesus Christianity increasingly becomes out of place in a secular society. Projections suggest that by 2040-2050, atheism and Islam could outnumber Our Lord Jesus Christianity. That is why unity is paramount – standing together, hand in hand, and refraining from internal conflicts.

This parable carries five important spiritual lessons:

A. Unity and Harmony: The primary message is the importance of unity and harmony. Just as a kingdom or house divided against itself cannot stand, so too is the need for unity within the Church and among believers. The Church is often referred to as the Body of Our Lord Jesus Christ, and division within it weakens its ability to fulfil its mission. The metaphor of the Church as the Body of Christ emphasizes the interconnectedness of its members. In the New Testament, particularly in the writings of the Apostle Paul, believers are described as different parts of one body, each with a unique function but working together for the overall health and purpose of the body (1 Corinthians 12:12-27). This imagery underscores the significance of unity among believers that can only navigate the church from strength to strength;

1. Fulfilment of Mission:
   – A united Church can effectively carry out its mission of spreading the Gospel and embodying the

teachings of Christ. When believers are in harmony, they can collectively impact the world with the message of love, redemption, and salvation.

2. Strength in Diversity:
   - The diversity of gifts, talents, and perspectives within the Church is a source of strength when harnessed together. Unity does not mean uniformity; rather, it involves appreciating and celebrating the differences among believers while working toward shared goals.

3. Witness to the World:
   - Unity within the Church serves as a powerful witness to the world. When outsiders see a community of believers living in harmony, despite their differences, it reflects the transformative power of Christ's teachings and attracts others to explore the Christian faith.

4. Resilience in Challenges:
   - A united Church is better equipped to face challenges, both internal and external. Whether dealing with internal conflicts or addressing external pressures, a cohesive community can withstand adversity with a collective spirit of love, forgiveness, and support.

5. Reflecting God's Nature:
   - Unity within the Church mirrors the unity found in the Trinity nature of God—the Father, the Son Jesus Christ, and the Holy Spirit. The oneness among believers reflects the divine unity and serves as a testament to the transformative work of the Holy Spirit in their lives.

6. Preserving Doctrinal Integrity:

- Unity is crucial in preserving the doctrinal integrity of the Church. When disagreements arise, a unified approach to resolving theological issues ensures that the core tenets of the faith remain intact, preventing the dilution of essential Christian teachings.

A. Spiritual Warfare: The parable also speaks to the broader concept of spiritual warfare. Orthodox Christianity acknowledges the existence of spiritual forces of darkness, and unity among believers is essential in resisting these forces.

B. Church Unity: Early Church Fathers emphasized the importance of unity within the Church. Saint Ignatius of Antioch, an early Christian writer, stressed the need for unity among believers and obedience to the bishop. He wrote, *"Where the bishop is to be seen, there let all his people be; just as wherever Our Lord Jesus Our Lord Jesus Christ is present, there is the universal Church"* (Letter to the Ephesians).

C. Love and Forgiveness: The parable also invites reflection on the importance of love and forgiveness within the Our Lord Jesus Christian community. Divisions often arise from conflicts and grievances, and practicing love and forgiveness is essential for maintaining unity.

D. Proclaiming Oneness: It is crucial to acknowledge that the seeds of schism and departure from the Church's unity are sown at the local level we mean the very basic level of one family, one church, one diocese. The onset of heresy and subsequent schism typically originates with disagreements within a local congregation. This disagreement leads to disputes, a hardening of hearts, and ultimately, the formation of a separate group. The Fathers opposed schism not only for theological reasons but also because they perceived it as a failure to embody love. While we must avoid allowing local conflicts to escalate into schism or the creation of new churches, engaging in loveless quarrelling still has detrimental effects on our souls. Following Saint James' advice, *"So then, my beloved brethren, let every man be swift to hear, slow to speak, slow to wrath"* (James 1:19) within our local congregations. Charity, both in almsgiving and ecclesial unity, begins at home. Confessing belief in one church necessitates embracing the responsibility to love, forgive, and promptly resolve disputes. Only through these actions can love become the perfect bond of unity, upholding the unity of the Spirit in the bond of peace

In summary, the call for unity and harmony within the Church is not just a practical necessity; it is deeply rooted in the theological understanding of the Church as the Body of Christ. A united Church is better positioned to fulfil its mission, draw strength from its diversity, bear witness to the world, navigate challenges, reflect Christ's nature, and preserve the integrity of its doctrinal foundation.

Chapter 5

The Parable of the Sower and the Seed

This parable comes from the Gospel of Saint Matthew 13:1-23.

"On the same day Our Lord Jesus went out of the house and sat by the sea. And great multitudes were gathered together to Him, so that He got into a boat and sat; and the whole multitude stood on the shore. Then He spoke many things to them in parables, saying: 'Behold, a sower went out to sow. And as he sowed, some seed fell by the wayside; and the birds came and devoured them. Some fell on stony places, where they did not have much earth; and they immediately sprang up because they had no depth of earth. But when the sun was up they were scorched, and because they had no root they withered away. And some fell among thorns, and the thorns sprang up and choked them. But others fell on good ground and yielded a crop: some a hundredfold, some sixty, some thirty. He who has ears to hear, let him hear!' And the disciples came and said to Him, 'Why do You speak to them in parables?' He answered and said to them, 'Because it has been given to you to know the mysteries of the kingdom of heaven, but to them it has not been given. For whoever has, to him more will be given, and he

The Parable of the Sower and the Seed

will have abundance; but whoever does not have, even what he has will be taken away from him. Therefore I speak to them in parables, because seeing they do not see, and hearing they do not hear, nor do they understand. And in them the prophecy of Isaiah is fulfilled, which says: "Hearing you will hear and shall not understand, And seeing you will see and not perceive; For the hearts of this people have grown dull. Their ears are hard of hearing, And their eyes they have closed, Lest they should see with their eyes and hear with their ears, Lest they should understand with their hearts and turn, So that I should heal them."

But blessed are your eyes for they see, and your ears for they hear; for assuredly, I say to you that many prophets and righteous men desired to see what you see, and did not see it, and to hear what you hear, and did not hear it. 'Therefore hear the parable of the sower: When anyone hears the word of the kingdom, and does not understand it, then the wicked one comes and snatches away what was sown in his heart. This is he who received seed by the wayside. But he who received the seed on stony places, this is he who hears the word and immediately receives it with joy; yet he has no root in himself, but endures only for a while. For when tribulation or persecution arises because of the word, immediately he stumbles. Now he who received seed among the thorns is he who hears the word, and the cares of this world and the deceitfulness of riches choke the word, and he becomes unfruitful. But he who received seed on the good ground is he who hears the word and understands it, who indeed bears fruit and produces: some a hundredfold, some sixty, some thirty.'"

The Parable of the Sower and the Seed is a straightforward yet a profound lesson about the Kingdom of Heaven. Our Church revisits this parable on multiple occasions, particularly during the first two Sundays of the month of Hatour. It holds remarkable power for our life's journey. As we traverse life's various stages, our heart might resemble the wayside where birds readily snatch away God's words, which our Lord scatters our way through scriptures, sermons, meditation, or even during confession, guided by our spiritual father. This is the heart of arrogance, which is made vulnerable to Satan's advances through pride—an exposed heart with no defensive walls and undisciplined senses. Such a heart bears no fruit. If this describes our own hearts, we must beseech the Lord saying, "Rebuild the walls of Jerusalem!"

At other points in life, our heart might mimic a stony path—shallow, superficial, a heart of hypocrisy. This is a deceitful heart, cloaking its rocky nature beneath a facade of glamour. This heart embraces the Word, seeking to please all, but its inner hypocrisy corrodes the living message. This heart cannot endure the sun's rays or the light, as they expose its inner truth. It prefers the darkness of h.

Then come seasons when our heart strays from God, entangled in worldly concerns, worries, and wealth. The world is deceptive. The more we cling to it, the more it offers us worldly, earthly gains—greater riches, more money, enhanced power, heightened prestige. Are these wrong? No. As Saint John Chrysostom once stated, *"Do not blame these things, but rather blame the corrupt mind."* We can possess these things, yet all must belong to God for His glory.

And then there is the good heart—the humble heart that submits to the sanctity of repentance, confessing to a spiritual father, purifying itself. It is the good ground, the ground of tears that flow with repentance, nourished with the powerful reforming edifying words of God, the tears of prayer and the waters of the Holy Spirit that shine within us—the sun of Our Lord Jesus Christ's righteousness—yielding abundant fruit.

When the living word of God is sown in the sinful nature of fallen man, a new life springs up. The ability to receive the word of God is given to all people without exception, and the chance to receive this new life from hearing the word of God is given to everyone to the same extent. The fundamental concern of the whole of Christian life consists in constantly working on one's own heart to prepare the ground in oneself for receiving the seed (the word) of God. Men approach this task in different ways. While we explain the meaning of the Parable of the Sower, let each of us; in accordance with the words of Bishop Theophan the Recluse "...judge for himself as to which category he belongs."

Individuals who lack attentiveness, exhibit scattered thoughts, and lack reverence for the words of God resemble beaten paths where no fruitful growth is possible. The seeds of Divine wisdom fall on the coarse soil of souls trodden down by passions, thoughts, and vices. Their hearts, akin to a well-travelled road, are receptive to various impressions and thoughts, constantly seeking new allurements and amusements. In such minds, every virtuous thought is swiftly trampled by a flood of new impressions. During the exposure to the word of God, the enemy of salvation clandestinely steals away the divine message, as expressed by the holy Saint John of Kronstadt, likening it to a thief robbing a negligent homeowner. Consequently, the word of God quickly fades from their memory, forgotten as if never heard.

According to Scripture, the Kingdom of God springs up in a man unnoticed and miraculously, akin to the growth of the seed in the parable. The fruits of this Kingdom manifest in us mysteriously, and we may not quantify their increase. However, when our hearts burn within us, akin to the disciples at Emmaus, it signifies that the Lord is opening our minds to understand the Scriptures and revealing the mysteries of His Kingdom within. When our focus shifts from learning about God through the Gospel to experiencing Him within ourselves, it indicates that the seed has borne fruit. The Parable of the Sower concludes with the words, *"He who has ears to hear, let him hear!"* Christ, through these words, seems to be knocking at the heart of every individual, urging us to introspect, understand ourselves, and identify the category of people mentioned earlier to which we belong.

Finally, in the Parable of the Sower, our Lord Christ presents a universal goal for all: to receive the word of God wholeheartedly, embracing it with a pure and virtuous heart.

The concept of a pure heart finds powerful expression in the words of the Apostle Saint Paul, who proclaimed, *"it is no longer I who live, but Christ lives in me*; (Galatians 2:20).

To allow the word of God to take deep root within us, we must cultivate our hearts like a wise farmer tending to the soil, removing the thorns and weeds through repentance. This spiritual transformation, described by Saint Gregory the Theologian as a *"Divine change,"* regenerates the very essence of our being.

The Parable of the Sower emphasizes that God's salvation requires active participation from individuals. The Lord, as the Sower, implants His life-creating word in each heart, necessitating the openness and acceptance of this divine message to yield fruitful outcomes.

In the Lord's Prayer, as we entreat, *"Thy Kingdom come, Thy will be done, on earth as it is in heaven,"* Christ underscores that the sought-after kingdom is within. However, this kingdom, in line with Christ's teaching, is realized through exertion. The Lord anticipates human initiative—a dynamic commitment to active service to God and neighbour, coupled with the earnest pursuit of personal perfection.

Let us raise our voices, beseeching the Lord to transform our core desire, making it essential to wholeheartedly follow Him and bear fruits that glorify His name.

Come, Lord, and conquer the death within us, fill us with Your love, envelop us in Your love, let us taste this love, and lead us to follow You. Let Your Holy Spirit labour within us, yielding fruit a hundredfold for Your glory.

Chapter 6

The Parable of the Wheat and the Tares

    This parable is from the Gospel of St Matthew 13:24-30, and it is known as the Parable of the Wheat and the Tares. It reads as follows: *"Another parable He put forth to them, saying: 'The kingdom of heaven is like a man who sowed good seed in his field; but while men slept, his enemy came and sowed tares among the wheat and went his way. But when the grain had sprouted and produced a crop, then the tares also appeared. So the servants of the owner came and said to him, "Sir, did you not sow good seed in your field? How then does it have tares?" He said to them, "An enemy has done this." The servants said to him, "Do you want us then to go and gather them up?" But he said, "No, lest while you gather up the tares you also uproot the wheat with them. Let both grow together until the harvest, and at the time of harvest I will say to the reapers, "First gather together the tares and bind them in bundles to burn them, but gather the wheat into my barn."* Then the Disciples asked Our Lord Jesus: *"Explain to us the parable of the tares of the field."* He answered and said to them: *"He who sows the good seed is the Son of Man. The field is the world, the good seeds are the sons of the kingdom, but the tares are the sons of the wicked one. The enemy who sowed them is the devil, the harvest is the end of the age, and the reapers are the angels. Therefore as the tares are gathered and burned in the fire, so it will be at the end of this age. The Son of Man will send out His angels, and they will gather out of His kingdom all things that offend, and those who practice lawlessness, and will cast them into the furnace of fire. There will be wailing and gnashing of teeth. Then the righteous will shine forth as the sun in the kingdom of their Father. He who has ears to hear, let him hear!"*

Our Lord Jesus often used simple stories to teach about the Kingdom of Heaven. We are the sons and daughters of the Kingdom. Our focus should remain fixed on the Kingdom of Heaven, and we must avoid straying from this path. Our Lord Our Lord Jesus pointed out, *"For what profit is it to a man if he gains the whole world, and loses his own soul?"* (Matthew 16:26). Losing one's soul includes also forfeiting God's Kingdom. This parable has inspired countless sermons and touched the hearts of millions.

In the preceding parable of the Sower and the seed, the focus was on the diverse ways individuals receive and respond to the word of God. This narrative delved into the varied effects of the divine message on people. Transitioning to the parable of the wheat and the tares, Christ directs attention to the fourth portion of seed that fell on good ground, exploring how the enemy of human salvation strategically seeks to undermine the growth within this fertile soil. This parable carries significant relevance in our contemporary era, where the origin of evil in the world becomes a subject of inquiry, and individuals grapple with perplexities surrounding temptations, schisms, and defections within the Church. It serves as a guiding narrative to address questions about the sources of Church temptations, their underlying causes, and the forces that inspire them.

After narrating the parable, our Lord Christ provides an elucidation to both the disciples and us, identifying Himself as the Sower of the good seed, the Son of Man. In this spiritual analogy, the devil is depicted as the adversary, responsible for sowing the tares or weeds. The expansive field represents the world, encompassing Christ's universal Church. The good seed symbolizes the sons of the Kingdom, individuals within the Church who have embraced the grace-filled seed of God's word, transforming them into virtuous wheat destined for the heavenly kingdom. Conversely, the tares signify the offspring of the evil one—false teachers and tempters—agents through whom Satan carries out his destructive agenda.

The wisdom of the Church Fathers underscores the devil's persistent opposition to Christ. Saint John Chrysostom notes the pattern of false prophets emerging after the true prophets, false apostles following the Apostles, and anticipates the eventual appearance of Antichrist after Christ. Our Lord Christ's divine call to truth contrasts sharply with the devil's deceitful tactics, wherein his agents disseminate destructive falsehoods and vices, camouflaging them with semblances of truth and goodness. This deceptive strategy earns these individuals the appellation of "tares," mirroring the external appearance of wheat. As Saint John Chrysostom points out, the devil resorts to sowing his own seed when thwarted in his attempts to steal, choke, or scorch the rooted truth.

Let both grow together until the harvest

Our Lord Christ's directive, *"Let both grow together until the harvest,"* signifies a profound truth articulated by Saint Augustine, who asserts that the Church, until the end of the age, will coexist with both the good and the evil without detriment to the righteous. The presence of tares within the Church should not undermine our faith and love. Saint Augustine emphasizes that our focus should be on cultivating our individual virtue, striving to be the metaphorical wheat. One of the early Orthodox Church fathers further illuminates this idea, drawing parallels to individuals like Saint Matthew (formerly a despised tax collector) and figures like Saint Paul and the right-hand thief. If prematurely removed when they were considered tares, the virtuous contributions emerging from their transformative journeys would have been lost. This underscores the enduring potential for positive change and growth within individuals, emphasizing the importance of patience and discernment within the Church community.

Our Lord Jesus Christ, in His merciful intentions, seeks not the demise of sinners but their enlightenment, return and salvation, as expressed in *"who desires all men to be saved and to come to the knowledge of the truth."* (I Timothy 2:4). Through the warmth of His benevolence and the vivifying radiance of His love, He aims to soften hardened hearts, instigating a renewal, as highlighted in *"Therefore, if anyone is in Christ, he is a new creation; old things have passed away; behold, all things have become new."* (II Corinthians 5:17). The exemplary piety of His chosen becomes both an inspiration and a rebuke to those entrenched in sinful ways. Reflecting on the transformation of Saul, the persecutor of Christians prompts consideration: if Saul could become Paul, how many pagans embraced fervent faith witnessing the martyrs' selflessness?

The Holy Fathers liken the Church of Christ to Noah's ark, wherein there were clean and unclean animals together. Again, the Church is like a net in which various creeping things are also drawn in together with the fish. Various people both sinners and righteous make up the Church, the Body of Christ. There are in her people who have attained the height of spiritual perfection, and there are spiritual babes. It is necessary to take care of the beginners and not to tempt and repel them as weak members of the Church through "zeal not according to knowledge."

In our world, wheat and tares are always intertwined. Good and bad coexist. Think of examples like Cain and Abel, Esau and Jacob, Moses and Pharaoh, Saul and David, or even Alexander the Coppersmith, who caused considerable harm to Saint Paul *"Alexander the coppersmith did me much harm. May the Lord repay him according to his works."* (2 Timothy 4:14).

The Parable of the Wheat and the Tares conveys several significant spiritual lessons:

1. God's Patience and Judgment: The owner's decision to wait until the harvest reflects God's patience and longsuffering. God allows both the righteous and the unrighteous to coexist for a time, granting unceasing opportunities for repentance and redemption. However, a day of judgment will defiantly come when each will be separated according to their true nature.

2. Discernment and Not Judging Prematurely: The parable encourages discernment without hasty judgment. Our Lord Jesus Christian believers are called to exercise spiritual discernment and wisdom, recognizing the difference between good and evil, but refraining from condemning or uprooting others prematurely.

3. Eschatological Message: The Parable of the Wheat and the Tares carries an eschatological message, emphasizing the final judgment when God will separate the righteous from the wicked. Early Church Fathers often wrote about the importance of living with the expectation of Our Lord Jesus Christ's return and the final judgment. *Saint Ignatius of Antioch, an early Our Lord Jesus Christian writer, wrote in his Letter to the Ephesians: "For the last times have come upon us. Let us therefore be of a reverent spirit, and fear the long-suffering of God, that it tend not to our condemnation."*

4. Repentance, renewal and Transformation: While the parable acknowledges the existence of tares, it does not rule out the possibility of repentance and transformation. Some tares may turn into wheat through God's grace and mercy.

Our Lord Jesus warned us that, "*I send you out as sheep in the midst of wolves*" (Matthew 10:16). There will always be a Herod seeking to eliminate John the Baptist, or a tax collector praying next to a Pharisee. Our Lord Jesus proclaimed this truth. Moreover, within each of us exists both a side that seeks righteousness (wheat) and a side prone to imperfection (tares): the new man and the old.

Early on, wheat and tares resemble each other closely. But as they grow, differences emerge. Wheat develops a beautiful, productive head and nourishing fruit. Conversely, tares produce thorns that can be harmful. In Hebrew, these tares are called 'zonine,' which translates to 'pseudo wheat' The Arabic tradition refers to them as 'zawan,' recalling an old myth where wheat transformed into 'zawan' during the time of Sodom and Gomorrah.

Our Lord Jesus cautioned us about false prophets, saying, *"Beware of false prophets, who come to you in sheep's clothing"* (Matthew 7:15). Throughout history, false prophets have existed, like the story of Naboth's vineyard. Jezebel appeared devout initially, calling for fasting and prayer, but later revealed her sinister intentions to seize Naboth's vineyard. Similarly, Herod portrayed piety while seeking the Child from the Magi. His true intentions, however, contradicted this image. Only God can truly distinguish between wheat and tares. He knows each of us completely. It is crucial not to rush into judgment against others. We are not tasked with determining who will enter God's Kingdom. God examines the entire heart, understanding all things. He reminds us, *"Do not judge according to appearance but judge with righteous judgement"* (John 7:24). Saint Paul also says, *"Who are you to judge another's servant? To his own master he stands or falls. Indeed, he will be made to stand, for God is able to make him stand"* (Romans 14:4). God, the Almighty, never sleeps. *"He who keeps Israel shall neither slumber nor sleep"* (Psalm 121:4). Even in the Epistle to Philemon, Onesimus transitioned from a tare to wheat through his encounter with Saint Paul. Our hidden actions will eventually come to light.

Saint John the beloved wrote in his gospel *"That the light has come into the world, and men loved darkness rather than light, because their deeds were evil"* (John 3:19). Today, God calls us to be wheat in the world, as sons and daughters of His Kingdom. This is our purpose, and the ultimate judgment about tares rests with God, the Just Judge. It is not our role to eradicate the "weeds." Our Lord Jesus Christ instructs us to let both grow together. Our task is to flourish like wheat, bearing fruits in multiples of thirty, sixty, and a hundred. As Our Lord Jesus Christians, we must bear fruit and not waste energy uprooting what we think are "tares. Our Lord Jesus Christ's time on Earth focused on building, establishing principles, and inspiring His believers to spread His teachings.

Satan attempts to distract us with problems and mistakes. This drains our energy and inner peace. We might lose our smiles and our love and replace them with anger and judgment toward others. However, this is not our mission. The most effective way to address tares is by setting a positive example. *Benjamin Franklin wisely noted, "Instead of cursing the darkness, light a candle."*

May God grant us all the ability to live as wheat in this world, radiating light?

Chapter 7

The Parable of the Mustard Seed

The Parable of the Mustard Seed: A Symbol of the Kingdom of Heaven

We continue our contemplation on the parables of the Kingdom of Heaven, delving into Saint Matthew 13:31: *"The kingdom of heaven is like a mustard seed, which a man took and sowed in his field, which indeed is the least of all the seeds; but when it is grown it is greater than the herbs and becomes a tree, so that the birds of the air come and nest in its branches."*

We encounter the parable of the mustard seed in three of the Evangelists: Matthew (13:31-32), Mark (4:30-32) and Luke (13:18-19). Our reflections centre on the Kingdom of God and eternal life. In our lives, Heaven holds the utmost significance. Our Lord Jesus Christ consistently initiated His teachings with, *"The Kingdom of heaven is at hand"* (Matthew 3:2). During the Last Supper, He told His disciples that, *"I am going to prepare a place for you. And if I go and prepare a place for you, I will come again and receive you to Myself; that where I am, there you may be also."* (John 14:2-3). And again in His last moments, He prays saying, *"Father, I desire that they also, whom You gave me, may be with Me"* (John 17:24). These were His paramount concerns. His heart was focused on urging us toward the Kingdom: *"Seek first the kingdom of God and His righteousness"* (Matthew 6:33). Through the Parable of the Sower, Our Lord Jesus emphasized the importance of receptive hearts, likening them to soil, and using this analogy Satan's effort to disturb the growth of faith and righteousness within us.

The Mustard Seed and the Tares: Contrasting Perspectives on Salvation

In this parable, it is crucial to grasp that Christ is drawing a comparison between the Kingdom of Heaven and the mustard seed, not emphasizing its small physical size (as there was a saying among the Jews: "Small as a mustard seed" but highlighting the ultimate process of its growth into a substantial, bushy tree that provides shelter for flocks of birds. Here, birds serve as a metaphor representing the people of God, finding refuge (salvation) in the Church of Christ that was destined to be established. The seemingly lifeless and minute mustard seed, declared the least among all seeds in the parable, symbolizes the profound mystery of resurrection from the dead.

The collocation of Jesus's parables holds a purposeful connection, particularly when the mustard seed parable follows the discourse on tares. This strategic placement is not coincidental; instead, it weaves a thematic thread between them. The parable of the sower establishes that only a fourth part of the sown seed perseveres and flourishes, representing those who find salvation. However, the subsequent parable of the tares introduces a significant peril that extends even to this fourth part of the sown seed.

As the disciples absorb these parables, the potential despair arising from the realization of a relatively small number destined for salvation might have overwhelmed them. Acknowledging this concern, the Lord provides additional parables—the mustard seed and the leaven. The mustard seed, despite its minuscule size, transforms into the greatest among herbs, evolving into a tree where birds find shelter in its branches.

This metaphorical narrative extends to the realm of Christian preaching. Similar to the mustard seed, the Christian message, initially modest, burgeons into a force of profound impact. The disciples, seemingly powerless by human standards, house great, concealed power within them. This latent power propels the Gospel's dissemination, transcending geographical boundaries and cultural barriers, ultimately spreading throughout the entire world.

In essence, the mustard seed parable reassures the disciples that, just as the smallest seed can grow into the mightiest tree, their seemingly humble efforts, infused with divine power, will significantly influence the world.

Earthly Distractions and the Call to Focus on Eternal Life

I would like to share my perspective: the tares sown by Satan when we are distracted distort our perception of eternal life. Satan deliberately confuses humanity, prompting an obsession with earthly matters. The idea of heaven or the Kingdom has become unpopular, and death is increasingly dreaded. Many feels entitled to the earth, living as if immortality was guaranteed here. It is this mindset which has been quietly embedded in our minds overtime that has distorted our vision of eternal life. Satan sows these tares when we are young and reaps the fruit of diverting us from the eternal path.

In the Church, our focus should revolve around eternal life, our ultimate destination. Yet, we find ourselves occupied with other subjects. The Church's central message should steer us toward eternity and guide us from a worldly perspective to a divine one. These perspectives stand in clear opposition, as illustrated by the story of the rich man and Lazarus. In worldly eyes, the rich man is esteemed, whereas the heavenly perspective values Lazarus. The Church's duty is to nurture and equip us for eternity.

The Power of Small Beginnings: Examples of Spiritual Growth

This parable beautifully portrays spiritual growth in reaching the Kingdom. Have you seen a mustard seed? It is minuscule, like a tiny particle of dust God, however, prefers to work with mustard seeds. The Prophet Samuel was such a seed and blossomed into prominence among the Jews. David, initially a mustard seed, bloomed into a great tree, bearing Psalms. Joseph the Righteous, another mustard seed, became a towering tree of wisdom; a saviour of humanity. Long ago, a "mustard seed" named Boulos Ghabriel transformed into a virtuous giant tree, Bishop Abraam of Fayoum and Giza, sheltering countless impoverished souls. Habib Girgis, once a mustard seed, catalysed the Sunday school movement in the Coptic Church. Nazir Gayed, a mustard seed, grew into a towering tree, shepherding millions as Pope Shenouda III for decades. Father Mina Nematalla, a mustard seed planted in Australia, propagated into a vast tree serving generations. Never underestimate the potential of a small mustard seed; God can cultivate something grand from it. The widow's two coins hold immeasurable value.

The mustard tree, flourishing in the warmth of regions like Judea, reaches remarkable dimensions that distinguish it from mustard plants in other parts of the world. Unlike the modest shrub-like stature of its counterparts, the Judean mustard tree grows to towering heights. Its branches provide ample shade, allowing a man on horseback to pass beneath them. Furthermore, these robust branches find utility in fuelling large furnaces, displaying the versatility and strength inherent in the tree. Even the weight of a man does not break its branches, and flocks of birds find refuge on its expansive boughs. Additionally, the medicinal properties attributed to the seeds contribute to the widespread recognition of the mustard tree.

Christ as the Mustard Seed and Sower: The Source of the Church's Strength

In drawing parallels between the mustard tree and Christ, the analogy becomes poignant and profound. Christ, identified as both the mustard seed and the Sower, embodies the essence of the entire Church. Like the mustard seed containing the potential for expansive growth within its small form, Christ encapsulates the entirety of the Church within Himself. He serves as the eternal Head of the Church, underscoring its dependence on Him for existence. Without Christ, the Church would cease to be.

Christ, as the Sower, willingly embraces death as a transformative act. Through this sacrificial act, He imparts life to His Church, extending the gift of salvation to all who believe in Him. This selfless act finds resonance in Christ's own words: *"Most assuredly, I say to you, unless a grain of wheat falls into the ground and dies, it remains alone; but if it dies, it produces much grain."* (John 12:24). Here, our Lord Christ metaphorically likens Himself to a grain of wheat whose sacrifice leads to the abundant fruition of life.

In essence, the imagery of the mustard tree and Christ's role as the mustard seed and Sower beautifully encapsulates the transformative power of His sacrifice, the enduring strength of the Church, and the expansive reach of His redemptive message.

The Journey of the Mustard Seed: Spiritual Transformation and Nurturing Faith

For the mustard seed to bear fruit, consider its journey. It is first buried, as we must kill our ego and accept our mortality. Then it is watered with the tears of prayers, learning, and the Holy Spirit is presence. It is compressed, enduring pressure, like being trampled upon. Finally, the small seedling emerges above the soil.

The analogy between the mustard seed and the grace-filled word of God extends to the notion of warmth and nourishment. Just as the mustard seed produces warmth, the transformative power of the word of God, when received by the heart, kindles spiritual warmth within. This warmth is not merely physical but a profound, grace-filled experience that touches the core of one's being.

The Gospel of Luke recounts a poignant example of this spiritual warmth. Cleopas and another disciple were walking to Emmaus, disheartened after the crucifixion of Jesus. In their encounter with the risen Christ, they later reflected, *"Did not our heart burn within us while he talked with us on the road"* (Luke 24:32)? This burning sensation symbolizes the transformative effect of the grace-filled word of God, igniting a fervent passion and understanding within the disciples' hearts.

Furthermore, the analogy draws parallels between the mustard seed's ability to stimulate an appetite for food and the word of God's capacity to awaken a spiritual hunger. Just as the mustard seed creates a desire for physical nourishment, the word of God prompts a soulful craving for the Heavenly Bread—Christ Himself. This hunger extends beyond mere physical sustenance; it encompasses a profound thirst for salvation and justification in Christ the Saviour.

In essence, the mustard seed serves as a tangible metaphor for the transformative and nourishing qualities inherent in the word of God. Both produce warmth that penetrates the heart and an appetite that stirs a spiritual hunger for the divine. This interplay of metaphorical elements deepens the understanding of the transformative power of God's grace-filled message.

Embracing the Mustard Seed Within: Endurance and Spiritual Growth

When life brings immense pressure and stress, do not despair. God is nurturing buds from the tiny seed within you. Recognize your role as a mustard seed prepared to flourish into a mighty tree. Understand what is required and surrender to His guidance, as stated in (1 Corinthians 3:7): *"So then neither he who plants is anything, nor he who waters, but God who gives the increase"*

Beloved brethren, when life presses you and tears flow, they water the seed inside, allowing it to grow. God's plan is for us to share in His Kingdom. Comprehend your purpose during your earthly existence. Nurture your mustard seed, vigilantly staying focused on growth and embracing your journey. Keep your eyes fixed on Heaven and eternity, for this is paramount in life.

May God bless us all with fruitfulness and progress in virtuous deeds, aiding us in comprehending our purpose on Earth?

Chapter 8

The Parable of the Leaven

The Parable of Leaven: A Hidden Transformative Power

We continue our exploration of the Kingdom's parables with another from Our Lord Jesus Christ: *"Another parable He spoke to them: "The kingdom of heaven is like leaven, which a woman took and hid in three measures of meal till it was all leavened." All these things Our Lord Jesus spoke to the multitude in parables; and without a parable He did not speak to them, that it might be fulfilled which was spoken by the prophet, saying: "I will open My mouth in parables; I will utter things kept secret from the foundation of the world"* (Matthew 13:33-35).

Once again, a simple parable carries profound meaning. We have already discussed the Parable of the Sower, examining our resemblance to the different types of soil. Similarly, we have explored the concepts of wheat and tares, acknowledging the devil's interference, and the growth potential portrayed by the mustard seed, nurtured by grace.

Leaven: A Double-Edged Metaphor of Influence

In the teachings of our Lord Jesus, we encounter the intriguing metaphor of leaven on two distinct occasions, each carrying contrasting implications. Initially, in Matthew 13, our Lord Jesus employs the analogy to illustrate the nature of the kingdom of God. Later, in Matthew 16, our Lord Jesus warns His disciples about the deleterious influence of the Pharisees and Sadducees, likening it to leaven.

The first mention, found in (Matthew 13:33), depicts the kingdom of God as akin to leaven, subtly yet pervasively transforming its surroundings. This imagery suggests that the impact of God's reign may not always be immediately apparent but has a gradual, pervasive effect, much like leaven working its way through dough. Here, leaven symbolizes a positive, transformative force.

Conversely, in (Matthew 16:5-12), our Lord Jesus cautions against the "leaven of the Pharisees and Sadducees," urging vigilance against their corrupting influence. This metaphor highlights the insidious nature of false teachings and hypocritical attitudes, likening them to leaven that permeate and corrupts the whole.

The Power of Subtle Transformation: Lessons from Leaven

Both instances underscore the importance of discernment and spiritual vigilance. Just as leaven subtly alters the composition of dough, beliefs, attitudes, and influences can subtly shape our lives and communities. The disciples' initial confusion over Jesus' warning emphasizes the need for discernment in distinguishing between beneficial and harmful influences.

Moreover, the metaphor of leaven prompts reflection on the nature of personal and communal transformation. Just as leaven works unseen within dough, believers are called to embody the principles of God's kingdom, effecting positive change in their spheres of influence. Conversely, they must guard against the infiltration of harmful ideologies and behaviours that undermine the integrity of faith communities.

Ultimately, the metaphor of leaven serves as a potent reminder of the power of influence, both for good and ill. As followers of Christ, we are called to embody the transformative principles of God's kingdom, actively resisting the corrosive influence of falsehood and sin. In doing so, we fulfil our role as salt and light in a world in need of redemption.

The Unseen Work of Grace: Yeast as a Symbol of Inner Transformation

In this parable, Our Lord Jesus employs the metaphor of yeast, introducing an additional layer by addressing our inner lives. Yeast's action within dough remains unseen, yet it is alive, active, and transformative. Though it is easy to envision yeast fermenting dough, Our Lord Jesus Christ's choice of this parable delves into the deep, yet simple process of change brought about by God's grace.

The meaning of the figurative comparison of the Kingdom of God with dough, raised by the action of yeast, is that in both instances a living, creative beginning is at work. The heavenly leaven the grace of the Divine Spirit, placed by the Saviour in the human souls which compose His Church the Kingdom of God on earth, determines the growth of their inner, spiritual life. And as the leavened dough rises until the leaven is mixed with it completely, so also the process of establishing the Kingdom of God will continue until all its true children enter into it

Faith in God's Transformative Power: The Core of the Church's Mission

In serving God within our Church, focusing on soul-winning, it is crucial to hold steadfast faith in our Lord's transformative power. This belief constitutes the foundation of our faith. Yet, like the unseen yeast, understanding the intricacies of God's work remains elusive to us.

The central focus of the Church's mission revolves around unwavering faith in her Bridegroom, Shepherd, and Redeemer: Our Lord Jesus Christ Her sacred responsibility entails guiding souls towards Our Lord Jesus Christ, facilitating their connection with Him for the ultimate purpose of establishing His Kingdom, both in the heavenly realm and on Earth.

Without unwavering faith, confidence, and conviction in Our Lord Jesus Christ's ability to transform souls, church servants risk weakening their resolve and veering away from their primary role as believers in God's power. Frequently, reliance on personal capabilities results in activities that appear church-oriented but lack spiritual substance, masked as "church-made."

The Call for Personal Encounter and Spiritual Revival

Church servants must possess a personal connection with Our Lord Jesus Christ, encountering Him on an individual level, experiencing His transformative power firsthand. As Saint Paul advises, *"Do not be conformed to this world, but be transformed by the renewing of your mind"* (Romans 12:2). Amid life's challenges, the presence of numerous tares, the devil's presence, and rapid technological advancements, Our Lord Jesus Christ, our guiding light, stands even stronger, loftier, and broader. He conquers death, fostering life. This is the lesson derived from the yeast parable: the internal, invisible work that brews and transforms the entire mixture.

Faith in Action: Following the Example of Saint Peter

I envision this as akin to the experience of Saint Peter, who, after a night of toiling and catching nothing, came face to face with his own weakness. Yet, he believed that though he failed, the Lord could fill the nets. He humbly declared, *"At Your word Lord, I will let down the net"* (Luke 5:5).

In this parable, our role is to serve as instruments chosen by God for His transformative work. We are likened to the yeast, and it is a privilege to play this chosen role. To fulfil this role effectively, we must embody the qualities of active and alive yeast. Living in perfect harmony with Our Lord Jesus Christ is crucial. By closely following Him, we attain true life, for, as (John 14:6) states, *"He is the way, the truth, and the life."*

The Impact of a Vibrant Spiritual Life

When our inner life is vibrant, sincere, and profound, the more effectively we can ferment the dough – and the more powerfully we testify to the power of God. Our ability to be a strong leaven arises from a robust prayer life and a steadfast relationship with Our Lord Jesus Christ, experiencing His constant presence. The more we repent and turn back to God, the more we are infused with God's Spirit. Our unity with fellow believers amplifies our sense of Our Lord Jesus Christ's presence in our service, lives, and families. This was the spirit of the early Church—vigilant, united, and prayerful. Such unity allowed the Holy Spirit to descend mightily, shaking the surroundings with the power of their prayers.

The Challenge of Spiritual Unity: A Call to Unceasing Prayer

It is a challenge these days to get servants to pray together. There is often resistance these efforts, leading to numerous excuses for non-attendance. This resistance reflects weak, or inactive yeast Events and gatherings can outwardly appear vibrant and energetic but are spiritually dead.

Father Bishoy Yassa, one of the revered fathers whom God have graced us with their presence in Australia, stands as a remarkable beacon. His life story unfolds against the backdrop of adversity during the period of President Anwar Sadat's imprisonment of dissidents on September 5, 1981. During this challenging time, where 1,536 individuals were detained for their perceived opposition, including clergy and laity of the Coptic Orthodox Church, Father Bishoy Yassa emerged as a resilient figure.

A Living Example of Transformative Faith: Father Bishoy Yassa

An exceptional and vibrant force, Father Bishoy embodies transformative yeast in the fabric of our community. His devotion to prayer is the cornerstone of his life, evident in the emphasis on prayers and their transformative power within his sermons and confessions. The Agpeya and the Holy Liturgy hold a central place in his daily existence, with prayer preceding and following every task, occurring anywhere and at any time. Reflecting his commitment to spiritual fellowship, he gathers church servants for prayer at his home every Monday night. Father Bishoy Yassa serves as living yeast that has not only fermented our collective spirit but has also catalysed profound transformations in numerous lives. I personally recall every Monday night; he gathers church servants at his own home for prayer meetings leading us for hours of praying the midnight prayer and handing us over an unforgettable curriculum of how a servant should serve demonstrating by practice the importance of living what we preach and the fact that our utmost role as servants of the Lord is to pray unceasingly? Absolute simplicity and fluency in demonstrating a living example by embodying the transformative power of faith and reflecting the teachings of Christ in his rich life.

The Call to Self-Examination and Spiritual Growth

Let us review our inner lives, prayers, repentance, and unity within our church community. May God bless us with abundant grace and blessings, enabling us to grow and serve as vibrant leaven, transforming the entire mixture.

To You belongs the glory and honour, now and forever. Amen

Chapter 9

The Parable of the Pearl

Today's parable is: *"Again, the kingdom of heaven is like treasure hidden in a field, which a man found and hid; and for joy over it he goes and sells all that he has and buys that field"* (Matthew 13:44).

Understanding the Kingdom of Heaven

Upon encountering this parable, it is natural to reflect on what the kingdom of heaven represents personally. For many, the concept may evoke images of celestial realms or future salvation. However, delving deeper, one might consider the kingdom of heaven as a present reality—a realm where God's reign is acknowledged and embraced in daily life.

To some, the kingdom of heaven embodies a state of inner peace and spiritual fulfillment, where one's heart is aligned with divine purposes and values. It may signify a community of believers united by love, compassion, and justice—a foretaste of the harmony and wholeness promised in eternity.

For others, the kingdom of heaven might symbolize a journey of transformation and growth—a continual process of becoming more like Christ and participating in God's redemptive work in the world. It may involve acts of service, generosity, and forgiveness that reflect the character of God's kingdom on earth.

Moreover, contemplating the kingdom of heaven invites introspection and self-examination. It prompts individuals to consider how their beliefs, attitudes, and actions align with God's kingdom commandments, values, and priorities. It challenges them to prioritize seeking God's will and righteousness above personal desires and worldly pursuits.

Ultimately, the kingdom of heaven holds different meanings for each person, shaped by their unique experiences, beliefs, and spiritual journeys. Yet, amidst this diversity, it remains a profound invitation—to live with purpose, integrity, and hope, rooted in the reality of God's reign both now and in the age to come.

Experiencing the Kingdom Guarantee

Beloved friends, during our earthly existence, we do not fully grasp the Kingdom of Heaven. This is because it operates on a distinct calculation, employs a different language, and defies description as we know it. Even the saints, privileged with revelations about its glory, struggled to articulate it.

Saint Paul captures this essence in (1 Corinthians 2:9): *"Eye has not seen, nor ear heard, nor have entered into the heart of man the things which God has prepared for those who love Him."* However, while on this earthly journey, we are granted a foretaste of what we can call "the kingdom guarantee."

Have you ever stood in the liturgy, eyes shut, ensnared in prayer, oblivious to your surroundings, casting aside worries and troubles? In those moments, captivated by God's presence, have you sensed the assurance of the kingdom's embrace?

Have tears of devotion welled up in your eyes during private prayer, making you acutely aware of God's presence? At such instances, enveloped in the warmth of divine closeness, you declare, "I desire nothing of this world." This is the kingdom guarantee.

Have you ever witnessed a smile light up someone's face or wiped away tears as you washed the feet of the needy or infirm? In those moments, sharing your abundance with someone lacking, you felt an overwhelming sense of contentment. This is the kingdom guarantee.

The Pearl: A Symbol of Christ

The language of the kingdom remains elusive while on earth because we are confined by our earthly bodies. The fallen body cannot fully perceive the Spirit; we merely experience a guarantee of the Spirit.

The parable under discussion introduces us to an individual who, driven by profound joy, sacrifices everything to acquire a priceless pearl. Who is this pearl? Who is the wise merchant making the radical choice to relinquish all possessions in pursuit of this pearl?

This pearl represents Our Lord Jesus Our Lord Jesus Christ—a treasure worth divesting everything for. He is eternal life. How do you evaluate this transaction? Is it a loss or a gain? From every angle, selling everything to possess Our Lord Jesus, the eternal Pearl, is the ultimate gain. A worldly mindset might see it as a loss, forgoing all worldly possessions for Our Lord Jesus.

However, without a doubt, when viewed comprehensively, Our Lord Jesus is the gateway to eternal life after we depart this world. It is an investment, not a loss. Without this invaluable Pearl – Our Lord Jesus – eternal life and the delights of God's Kingdom evade us. Without Him, we cannot access eternal life, regardless of how well we decorate our tombs. Ultimately, if we lack Our Lord Jesus, we will not see Our Lord Jesus.

This extraordinary pearl symbolizes faith in Our Lord Jesus Our Lord Jesus Christ, belief in His mission, *"Father, I desire that they also whom You gave Me may be with Me where I am, that they may behold My glory which You have given Me"* (John 17:24). Our joy is in beholding God's glory, which He ordained for us before the creation of the world.

Recognizing and Pursuing the Pearl

Today, let us fervently pray to attain this Pearl from the depths of our hearts. Numerous individuals pursued this, Pearl. Cornelius diligently searched, ultimately finding Peter and securing this priceless treasure. Similarly, Nicodemus approached Our Lord Jesus under the cloak of night, relentlessly seeking this precious Pearl.

We all possess this Pearl, freely bestowed upon us. Nevertheless, something is amiss if we fail to recognize its value. Engrossed in the pursuit of worldly matters, we often fail to appreciate the Pearl's magnitude. Despite possessing the treasure we ardently desire in life, we overlook it. We own the precious treasure, an immense Pearl, yet struggle to comprehend Our Lord Jesus' presence and worth. This lack of understanding deprives us of joy and an awareness of our spiritual riches. It is akin to a wealthy person living in poverty.

What is the solution to this dilemma?

We must make a deliberate decision. No one can make it on our behalf; it is a choice we must make individually. The decision entails viewing everything in our lives as trivial compared to the Pearl's value. It demands casting aside erroneous relationships, hatred, and sin that obstruct and agitate our hearts, impeding our purity. Fear not this decision, for you will not regret it; instead, you will rejoice. Remove any hindrance from your life to embrace Our Lord Jesus Christ, the fount of blessing, joy, goodness, holiness, and grace. He enriches our lives and hearts through the indwelling Holy Spirit. This explains why countless individuals renounced worldly possessions to acquire this priceless Pearl.

A Testimony of Sacrifice

Years ago, I knew a dear friend in Egypt. He possessed good wealth, resources, scientific university degree, and occupied a high-ranking engineering role in a prominent multinational medical company. However, his gaze perpetually remained fixed on the Kingdom. Joyful and constantly beaming, he discussed the Kingdom and Our Lord Jesus Christ's essential role in life. Over time, he relinquished everything and embraced monasticism. Initially, I mourned the loss cherished friend and a spiritual brother very Rev. Fr Wissa Anba Bishoy. I failed to comprehend his decision. Many years later, both of us adorned in black robes, our paths crossed once more. It dawned on me that he surrendered everything to gain the precious, invaluable Pearl—recognizing that nothing in this world could compare to being with Our Lord Jesus Christ.

In the book "Way of the Ascetics", by Tito Colliander (10 February 1904 – 21 May 1989) was a Finnish Eastern Orthodox Christian writer. We encounter a chapter under the title *"On the Pearl of Great Price"*. The author writes of the signs of finding the precious pearl: "…the deeper r you pressed into your own heart, the farther and higher you climbed out of yourself. The outward conditions of your life are the same: you wash dishes and care for the children; you go to work, draw your salary, and pay your taxes. You do everything pertaining to your external life as a person in a society, since there is no chance of leaving it. But you have resigned yourself. You have given away one thing in order to receive another.

"…and if I have Thee, what more do I ask on earth? Nothing, answers Saint John Climacus, but ceaselessly praying, silently to cling to Thee. Some are enslaved by riches,

The Parable of the Pearl

others by honour, still others by acquiring possessions; my only desire is to cling to God.

"Prayer, with all it contains of self-renunciation, has become your real life, which you keep up as though only for the sake of prayer. Walking with God (Genesis 6:9) is from now on the only thing that has real value for you, and it includes all heavenly and earthly events. For him who bears Christ within himself there is neither death nor illness or any earthly clamour; he has already stepped into eternal life, and that embraces everything.

"and should sleep by night and rise by day, and the seed should sprout and grow, he himself does not know how. For the earth yields crops by itself: first the blade, then the head, after that the full grain in the head. (Mark 4:27-28).

Allow me to earnestly ask, heart to heart, why delay making this decision? You are fully aware that no treasure surpasses this Pearl, Our Lord Jesus. *"As sorrowful, yet always rejoicing; as poor, yet making many rich; as having nothing, and yet possessing all things"* (2 Corinthians 6:10). In the absence of Our Lord Jesus, we are indeed impoverished. He is in all things. Do not delay; sell all to relish the Pearl in your life.

To You belongs the glory and honour, now and forever. Amen.

Chapter 10

The Parable of the Net

The parable of the dragnet is taken from Matthew 13: *"Again, the kingdom of heaven is like a dragnet that was cast into the sea and gathered some of every kind, which, when it was full, they drew to shore; and they sat down and gathered the good into vessels, but threw the bad away. So it will be at the end of the age. The angels will come forth, separate the wicked from among the just, and cast them into the furnace of fire. There will be wailing and gnashing of teeth"* (Matthew 13:47).

This simple parable provides us with the image of a net being cast into the sea. This net symbolises the Church's teachings or the living word of God in the Scriptures, which is thrown into the sea by the servants of the Church. The sea is the world with its many different races, cultures, and individual hearts. The goal of the fisherman is to gather as many fish as possible to sell and make a profit. Likewise, the goal of the Church is to gather as many souls as possible for Our Lord Jesus Christ

In this parable, Our Lord Christ focuses on what happens at the end of this process. The net has returned to shore, and the good must be separated from the bad. The angels come and sort the souls just like in the parable of the wheat and the tares.

The Sorting Process and God's Judgment

The Lord of Glory emphasized the sorting process at the end of the age, a profound aspect that resonates throughout the Holy Bible. As the early church Saint Augustine wisely observed, *"The Holy Scriptures are our letters from home."* In the contemporary landscape, numerous individuals tend to construct their own philosophies around the Word of God found in the Bible. Some lean towards interpreting its teachings merely as metaphors or symbols, thereby dismissing the fullness and gravity of its intended meaning.

In the parallel between the net and God's future judgment, a significant similarity emerges. When fish swim together in the vast sea, their individual qualities are challenging to discern. However, when the net is full and drawn to the shore, the fisherman effortlessly distinguishes between the good and the bad. Similarly, the Church of Christ on earth, comprises a diverse spectrum of individuals—enthusiastic Christians who diligently follow God's commandments, alongside those who are negligent and lukewarm, identifying as Christians in name only without a corresponding commitment to a godly life. In their collective existence, differentiating between them based on the quality of their spiritual life proves challenging. Yet, the conclusive and impartial judgment of God, anticipated at the end of time, will unequivocally unveil the distinction between the righteous and the sinners. In His discourse on the Judgment (Matthew 25:31-46), our Lord Jesus Christ articulates with utmost clarity the unfolding of this divine revelation.

Contrary to such interpretations, the Holy Bible is unequivocal on the matter of judgment. It stands as the living word of God, not a mere collection of metaphors but a dynamic guide for living life. To echo the sentiments of the early church father Tertullian, *"The Scriptures are the cisterns that hold the eternal fountain; draw therefore from them waters of perpetual life."* This living word proves effective and sharper than any two-edged sword, capable of piercing the soul and discerning the thoughts and intentions of the heart.

Try to visualise this parable, and consider the souls gathered in this net; some will be gathered to a good place and some, God forbid, will be thrown into another. We often like to ignore this reality, preferring only to listen to the more palatable teachings. However, it is vital for our understanding of salvation that we consider the entire picture and not cover up the facts. Our Lord Jesus Christ spoke about judgement on many occasions, and He warned us each time to not be among those who do not qualify.

The Transformative Power of God's Word

This net that is the Word of God, can change many souls. If we take the Bible and read it with all our heart and mind, and if we pray and ask for God's grace, the Holy Spirit can transform these words into living words, *"The words that I speak to you are spirit, and they are life"* (John 6:63) and *"Man shall not live by bread alone, but by every word that proceeds from the mouth of God"* (Matthew 4:4).

The commandments grow from being nice sentiments we think of once in a while into the energy that directs our lives. This is the life that the Gospel invites us to. I cannot get over this quote when I read it, it blew me away *"You Christians look after a document containing enough dynamite to blow all civilisations to pieces, turn the world upside down and bring peace to a battle-torn planet. But you treat it as though it is nothing more than a piece of literature."* — *Mahatma Gandhi*

This quote from Mahatma Gandhi resonates deeply because it challenges Christians to recognize the transformative power of the Gospel in their lives and in the world. It highlights the discrepancy between the immense potential of the teachings found in the Christian scriptures and the often superficial or indifferent way they are approached.

Gandhi's words serve as a wake-up call, urging Christians to view the Bible not merely as a collection of moral guidelines or historical narratives but as a dynamic force capable of reshaping societies and individuals. He emphasizes the explosive impact that living out the principles of love, justice, and forgiveness contained in the Gospel can have on humanity.

Moreover, Gandhi's critique calls attention to the disconnect between professed faith and lived experience. He challenges Christians to embody the radical message of Christ, to live lives of integrity and compassion that reflect the revolutionary essence of the Gospel.

Ultimately, Gandhi's quote serves as a reminder of the profound responsibility that comes with embracing the Christian faith—to engage with the Scriptures earnestly, to allow its truths to permeate every aspect of life, and to actively work towards the realization of its transformative vision for the world. There are many who meditate, many who teach, many who are philosophers, but the life they live is a shadow of what is being taught.

The message is simple and clear my dear friends; yes, there is a Judgement Day. There is a sorting and a separation of bad and good. Where am I? This is a heavy question, but a necessary one. The invitation is already sent: *"Rejoice because your names are written in heaven"* (Luke 10:20).

A Story of Humility and Self-Examination

Let us conclude these reflections with a story: God guided Saint Anthony to travel to Alexandria in Egypt to meet a very simple monk named Father Shenouda. Saint Anthony was talking to God asking, "Has anyone in this world reached my spiritual level?" He then heard a voice saying, "You have not yet reached the spiritual level of Father Shenouda." Saint Anthony decided to go to Alexandria in search of Father Shenouda. When the simple monk saw Saint Anthony approaching, his heart trembled and he met him with great love saying, "I do not deserve to receive the Star of the Wilderness." Saint Anthony asked him, "What is your spiritual gauge and how do you start your day?" The monk replied, "I start each day early and pray and before thanking God, I place all my sins before my eyes and say all will go to heaven because of their good deeds but I deserve eternal punishment because of my sins. I repeat the same words before I go to sleep at night." Saint Anthony said to him, "You are like a person who works with gold. You work in peace and calmness and due to your simple, pure thoughts you will enter heaven before me, who lives my life in the wilderness isolated from others but have not reached your level."

Our Lord Jesus called us to be saints because it is written, *"Be holy, for I am holy."* (1 Peter 1:16). We often think this calling is too far beyond our reach but remember this simple monk's prayer rule. Remember all your weaknesses before God each day, just as he did. Live in hope and joy of our Saviour Our Lord Jesus Our Lord Jesus Christ Thanking Him every day in everything you do.

To You is the glory and the honour, forever and ever. Amen.

Chapter 11

The Parable of the Heart
– Part 1

"When He had called the multitude to Himself, He said to them, 'Hear and understand: Not what goes into the mouth defiles a man; but what comes out of the mouth, this defiles a man.' Then His disciples came and said to Him, 'Do You know that the Pharisees were offended when they heard this saying?' But He answered and said, 'Every plant which My heavenly Father has not planted will be uprooted. Let them alone. They are blind leaders of the blind. And if the blind leads the blind, both will fall into a ditch.' Then Peter answered and said to Him, 'Explain this parable to us.'

So Our Lord Jesus said, 'Are you also still without understanding? Do you not yet understand that whatever enters the mouth goes into the stomach and is eliminated? But those things which proceed out of the mouth come from the heart, and they defile a man. For out of the heart proceed evil thoughts, murders, adulteries, fornications, thefts, false witness, blasphemies. These are the things which defile a man, but to eat with unwashed hands does not defile a man'" (Matthew 15:10-20).

The Heart in the Teachings of Our Lord Jesus Christ

This parable is repeated in the gospel as written by Saint Mark chapter 7 and delves into a crucial aspect of our spiritual journey: the heart. It is a profound topic that will be covered over two chapters due to its depth and centrality in the spiritual life.

The heart is the very core through which Our Lord Jesus Christ interacts with humanity. Throughout His teachings, Our Lord Jesus Christ urges us to safeguard our hearts and maintain their purity. *"Keep your heart with all diligence"* (Proverbs 4:23) advises. This underscores the importance of protecting our hearts.

The Importance of a Pure Heart

Our focus on the heart is justified because it is through the heart that we perceive God. *"Blessed are the pure in heart, for they shall see God"* (Matthew 5:8). The heart is akin to the laboratory of our spiritual life. When we pray, it is from the heart; when we forgive, it is from the heart; when we love, it is with our whole heart; when we rejoice, it is from the heart. Even in the liturgy, we implore, *"Fill our hearts with joy and grace."* Saint Basil Liturgy

The heart is the epicentre of love, kindness, emotions, and all feelings. It is where divine love ignites and kindles a fire within us. When we recite Psalm 51, we say, *"Create in me a clean heart, O God, and renew a steadfast spirit within me,"* We ought to pause and reflect on how these words affect our hearts.

A pure heart treads the path of holiness and finds tranquillity and joy in the Lord's presence. Even young children grasp the value of a pure heart. I once had a remarkable experience during confession with a third grader. When asked, "What is the best thing in your life?" he responded after a moment's thought without minimal hesitation, "My heart, Abouna." When I inquired why, he replied, "Because Our Lord Jesus is in my heart, so my heart is precious." This reaffirmed the wisdom in Our Lord Jesus Christ's words: *"I thank You, Father, Lord of heaven and earth, that You have hidden these things from the wise and prudent and have revealed them to babes"* (Matthew 11:25).

Loving God and Others with a Pure Heart

A pure heart, filled with divine love, remains open to God's love. The Lord becomes the focal point of our thoughts, minds, and spirits. Our Lord Jesus Christ affirmed this when asked about the greatest commandment: *"You shall love the Lord your God with all your heart, with all your soul, and with all your mind"* (Matthew 22:36-37). He also emphasized, *"He who has My commandments and keeps them, it is he who loves Me. And he who loves Me will be loved by My Father, and I will love him and manifest Myself to him"* (John 14:21). This implies that the Holy Spirit dwells joyfully in such a heart, revealing its innermost secrets.

To open our hearts to the love of God, we must also open our hearts to love others, especially our brethren. A pure heart, devoid of evil, actively strives to share God's love and assist others in kindling this divine love within their hearts. Saint John Chrysostom noted that the Bible does not merely state that good and merciful deeds suffice; it adds that the pure in heart shall see God. *"And you shall love the Lord your God with all your heart, with all your soul, with all your mind, and with all your strength.' This is the first commandment. And the second, like it, is this: 'You shall love your neighbour as yourself.' There is no other commandment greater than these."* (Mark 12:30-31)

The Connection Between Loving God and Loving Others

The connection between loving the Lord with all one's heart, mind, soul, and strength and loving one's brother as oneself lies in the essence of true devotion and compassion.

When a person loves the Lord with every fibre of their being—heart, mind, soul, and strength—they are acknowledging God's supreme authority and goodness in their lives. This love encompasses their emotional, intellectual, spiritual, and physical capacities, reflecting a complete surrender and dedication to God's will and commandments.

Simultaneously, this profound love for God inevitably spills over into how one interacts with others, particularly their brothers and sisters in humanity. When individuals genuinely love God, they recognize His love for all His creations, including every human being. Consequently, they are compelled to extend that same love, compassion, and respect to their fellow human beings.

In essence, loving one's neighbour as oneself is a natural outgrowth of loving God wholeheartedly. Just as individuals value their own well-being and happiness, they are called to value and prioritize the well-being and happiness of others. This love is not superficial or conditional but is rooted in a deep understanding of the inherent worth and dignity of every individual, regardless of differences or circumstances.

Thus, the connection between loving the Lord with all one's heart, mind, soul, and strength and loving one's brother as oneself lies in the unity of devotion, compassion, and empathy that emanates from a genuine relationship with God.

Anecdote: Guarding the Purity of the Heart

Let us conclude this discussion on the heart with an illustrative anecdote. I once encountered a married couple facing conflicts. Despite being active in church service, they exchanged negative and hurtful words. It is unfortunate

The Parable of the Heart (Part 1)

that sometimes, when people get deeply involved in church activities, they begin to lose respect for God's house. One day, I shared this situation with my spiritual father, and his response was sharp and clear: "Please forgive me do not fill my heart with this rubbish and pollute my ears." While initially uncomfortable and embarrassed by his reaction, it served as a potent reminder of the imperative to safeguard the purity of our hearts.

May God grant us the diligence to safeguard our souls and maintain the purity of our hearts.

To You belongs the glory and honour, now and forever. Amen.

Chapter 12

The Parable of the Heart
– Part 2

"When He had called all the multitude to Himself, He said to them, "Hear Me, everyone, and understand: There is nothing that enters a man from outside which can defile him; but the things which come out of him, those are the things that defile a man. If anyone has ears to hear, let him hear!"

When He had entered a house away from the crowd, His disciples asked Him concerning the parable. So He said to them, "Are you thus without understanding also? Do you not perceive that whatever enters a man from outside cannot defile him, because it does not enter his heart but his stomach, and is eliminated, thus purifying all foods?" And He said, "What comes out of a man, that defiles a man. For from within, out of the heart of men, proceed evil thoughts, adulteries, fornications, murders, thefts, covetousness, wickedness, deceit, lewdness, an evil eye, blasphemy, pride, foolishness. All these evil things come from within and defile a man." (Mark 7:14-23*).*

The Pure Heart

Continuing our exploration of the pure heart, we find that a pure heart is one that not only remains free from evil but is also untainted by evil desires and the love of sin. For such a heart to attain its full purity, it must be infused with love for God and righteousness. This infusion is the result of being filled with the Holy Spirit; no other source can achieve this transformation. Indeed, it is the Holy Spirit who has the power to change and fill the heart with divine love.

Purity is a divine gift bestowed by God upon those who ardently seek it, those who are committed to its pursuit, and those who labour to achieve it. Consider the example of Saint Abraam, the late Bishop of Fayoum and Giza. He was known for his ceaseless prayers and his repetition of the verse; *'Create in me a clean heart, O God, and renew a steadfast spirit within me'* (Psalm 51:10). He understood the truth that access to the Kingdom of God hinges upon possessing a pure heart.

The Immediate and Ultimate Goals

I would like to quote a remarkably interesting article wrote by Rev. Dr. Anthony Saint Shenouda, a Coptic Orthodox monk from Saint Shenouda Monastery in NSW, Australia. He completed his Master of Arts in Ancient History at Macquarie University, where he also completed his Doctor of Philosophy about the "Arrow Prayer in the Coptic Tradition." He is the Editor of Saint Shenouda Monastery Press. "Among the many themes that Saint John Cassian discusses with the desert fathers in his conference, is the theme of the attaining the purity of heart. In his first conference titled "on the purpose and goal of the monk" he asks the ultimate question, **"What is the purpose and end of the monastic life?"** The same question can be easily applied to the Christian life in general. This is the great and important question that we must turn to again and again throughout our life.

Abbot Moses, a hermit of Scetis answered, "we have come to the desert, to seek the kingdom of God, and the way to enter the kingdom is by achieving purity of the heart." Abba Moses further emphasised the very important idea of an immediate goal that a Christian must work at in order to successfully arrive to his final destination (i.e. the kingdom of heaven) explains that while the ultimate goal for a monk (and the same goes for all Christians) is to reign with Christ in heaven for eternity, Abba Moses suggests that "Christians need a closer target or goal to work at. This nearer goal is the purity of heart. "He illustrates the difference between the two goals with a practical example of a farmer who works the field day in and day out, not deterred with the changing weather, for the close goal of keeping the field free of weeds so as to attain the end goal of good harvest.

"All the arts and disciplines," he said, "have a certain 'scopus' or goal, and a 'telos,' which is the end that is proper to them, on which the lover of any art sets his gaze and for which he calmly and gladly endures every labor and danger and expense. For the farmer, avoiding neither the torrid rays of the sun one time nor the frost and ice another, tirelessly tills the soil and subdues the unyielding clumps of earth with his frequent ploughing, and all the while he keeps his scopos in mind: that, once it has been cleared of all the briers and every weed has been uprooted, by his hard work he may break the soil into something as fine as sand. In no other way does he believe that he will achieve his end, which is to have a rich harvest and an abundant crop."

This idea of the immediate goal and the ultimate goal is deeply rooted in the Bible, especially in the sermon on the mountain where Jesus said *"blessed are the pure in heart, for they shall see God"* (Matthew 5:8). By linking purity of heart to the vision of God, the beatitudes connects 'immediate goal' to 'end goal.'

The Parable of the Heart (Part 2)

Purity, Holiness, and Love

In the first conference Abba Moses equates the purity of heart to holiness. He even paraphrases the verse replacing "Holiness" with "Purity of Heart" and later on in the same conference he equates "Purity of Heart" to "Love," quoting Saint Paul: *"if I should give my goods to feed the poor and have not love it profits me nothing."* (1 Corinthians 13:3)

The common factor here between purity, holiness, and love is having an undivided heart. For Plato purity of heart meant clarity of purpose or freedom from disturbance. The word Holiness means set apart, or something that is only used for its intended purpose and Love as we know from the Old Testament cannot be divided "love the Lord your God with all your heart" and in the New Testament Christ gives the parable of the two masters "No one can serve two masters. For either he will hate the one and love the other, or else he will hold to the one and despise the other. You cannot serve God and mammon." (Mathew 6:24)

Having this undivided heart is what is meant by purity of heart there is so much in today's society that reaches out and grabs our attention from attaining our spiritual goal, study, career relationships, gadgets at discounted prices that claim to make our life easier meanwhile they sell us a way of life that makes us dependant on them. As Christians we must be watchful for any such distractions that drive out the love of Lord from our heart. Distractions are not necessarily doing evil, as we may imagine, but they can be ascetical works or church services when they become the aim rather than means as we will discuss later.

Now that we learned what purity of heart is, it is time to explore what it is not. From the above definition of purity of heart one might get the impression that it is an unattainable goal as some may confuse purity of heart with sinlessness, which is unattainable by human beings and even blasphemous to say so according to Saint John, *"If we say that we have not sinned, we make Him a liar"* (1 Jn 1:10). Our Lord also teaches us to pray in the Lord's Prayer to "forgive us our trespasses" this prayer He first taught to the holy and blessed apostles.

The purity of heart as Saint John Cassian sees it, is not a heart in a pristine state, unaffected and unscarred by sin but on the contrary, it is a heart that is fully alive despite and because of the scarce inevitably caused by sin."

This important article emphasizes the importance of having both an ultimate goal (reigning with Christ in heaven) and a closer, immediate goal (attaining purity of heart) in the Christian life. Purity of heart is equated with holiness and love, characterized by having an undivided heart devoted entirely to God. The article warns against distractions that can hinder spiritual growth and clarifies that purity of heart does not mean sinlessness but rather maintaining spiritual vitality despite the scars of sin.

Maintaining Purity of Heart

The Sacrament of Baptism initiates our spiritual renewal, but the journey to maintain purity demands unwavering effort. Without a pure heart, glimpsing the Kingdom of God remains unattainable. In our daily interactions, whether at work or in other settings outside our homes, we often face temptations that can lead us astray. However, the devoted Christian continually strives to preserve the purity of their senses. The Psalmist aptly states, *'Who may ascend into the hill of the LORD? Or who may stand in His holy place? He who has clean hands and a pure heart'* (Psalm 24:3-4). Our senses are the gateways to a pure heart. Our Lord emphasizes this, saying, *'The lamp of the body is the eye. Therefore, when your eye is good, your whole body also is full of light. But when your eye is bad, your body also is full of darkness. Therefore, take heed that the light which is in you is not darkness'* (Luke 11:34).

Those with a pure heart are privileged to behold God, not through their physical eyes, but through the illumination of their pure heart. Infused with divine grace, their spiritual eyes perceive God through the eyes of faith. Our Lord Jesus affirms, *'He who has My commandments and keeps them, it is he who loves Me. And he who loves Me will be loved by My Father, and I will love him and manifest Myself to him'* (John 14:21).

A pure heart neither harbors evil desires nor entertains anger, hatred, resentment, or revenge. Instead, it overflows with the love of the Lord. Its desires align with God's desires. The Book of Proverbs succinctly captures this truth, *'The desire of the righteous is only good'* (Proverbs 11:23).

Guarding the Heart

As Our Lord Jesus Christ refines the pure heart, it becomes a fortress against malicious thoughts, impurity, pride, and arrogance. From the heart, both goodness and wickedness spring forth. The heart serves as the wellspring of willpower and action, making its purification an essential endeavour.

A venerable Desert Father, Saint Agathon, astutely remarked, 'The struggle against the body's desires and its subjugation is akin to tending to the leaves of a tree. While important in preparing for the fruit, it does not imbue anyone with divine grace. However, the purification of the heart and mind resembles the delectable fruit that satisfies and nourishes the hungry. Indeed, purifying the heart is akin to cleansing the well that quenches the thirst of both the seeker and those they nurture.'

From an Orthodox perspective, purity of heart is foundational to the spiritual life. It encompasses a state of inner cleanliness and integrity, free from the contamination of sinful thoughts, desires, and motivations. In Orthodox theology, the heart is considered the center of a person's spiritual being, the place where one encounters God and cultivates communion with Him.

Purity of heart involves a continual process of purification, repentance, and transformation, guided by the grace of God and the practice of ascetic disciplines such as prayer, fasting, and almsgiving. It requires a sincere desire to align one's will with the will of God and to cultivate virtues such as humility, love, and compassion.

Orthodox spirituality emphasizes the importance of guarding the heart against the passions—destructive tendencies rooted in selfishness and sin, such as pride, greed, anger, lust, envy, gluttony, and sloth. These passions distort the soul and hinder its union with God, leading to spiritual blindness and bondage.

To attain purity of heart, Orthodox Christians are encouraged to engage in the sacramental life of the Church, participate in the services, receive the Holy Mysteries (Sacraments), and seek guidance from a spiritual father or mother. Through sincere confession and repentance, believers can experience the healing and forgiveness of Christ, allowing them to purify their hearts and live in communion with God.

The pursuit of purity of heart is not merely a personal endeavour but also a communal one. Orthodox Christians are called to cultivate love and unity within the Body of Christ, supporting and encouraging one another in the spiritual journey. By living in accordance with the commandments of Christ and following the example of the saints, believers can progress toward the goal of attaining purity of heart and experiencing the uncreated light of God's presence.

Attaining Purity of Heart

So, how can one attain purity of heart? Our spiritual forebears have offered guidance:

The Parable of the Heart (Part 2)

A contrite heart begets purity. This purity yields a tranquil heart, leading to humility—a virtue vital for a heart to become a dwelling place for God. The ego stands as the prime adversary of a pure heart. It renders the individual vulnerable to desires and fosters malicious thoughts toward others. To counteract this, the Desert Fathers advise frequent prayer, including the recitation of Psalms and concise prayers like the Our Lord Jesus Prayer. A particularly potent prayer, 'O My Lord Our Lord Jesus Christ, the Son of God, have mercy on me, a sinner,' can be repeated often in one's thoughts and heart. Another brief prayer that serves as an ideal prelude to daily activities is:

Our Lord Jesus, grant me a pure heart,

Our Lord Jesus, grant me a pure mind,

Our Lord Jesus, purify my eyes.

Try it; I assure you; it will yield amazing results.

Just as we cleanse a stained garment by immersing it in water and detergent, similarly, the Word of God purifies the heart. When we immerse our heart in the Holy Scriptures and frequently engage with its contents, we will be astonished by the transformation. Our heart will become as innocent as a child's, our vision purified, and our yearning to abide with Our Lord Jesus Christ deepened.

Great Saint Ephraim the Syrian prayed, *'O God, create within me a heart that is pure, chaste, unsullied, and simple. A heart that shuns evil thoughts, a heart of love, seeking peace and security for all. A heart that loves fasting, prayer, vigilance, self-abasement, humility, tranquillity, joy, and cheerfulness. A heart that loves charitable acts, assisting the needy, and nurturing others. O Lover of humanity, bestow upon me such a heart and instil Your unwavering steadfastness.'*

My Lord, on this day, grants us the gift of a pure heart, enabling us to embody genuine faith and witness Your Glory. To You belongs the glory and honour, now and forever. Amen

Chapter 13

The Parable of the Lost Sheep

"Take heed that you do not despise one of these little ones, for I say to you that in heaven their angels always see the face of My Father who is in heaven. For the Son of Man has come to save that which was lost "What do you think? If a man has a hundred sheep, and one of them goes astray, does he not leave the ninety-nine and go to the mountains to seek the one that is straying? And if he should find it, assuredly, I say to you, he rejoices more over that sheep than over the ninety-nine that did not go astray. Even so it is not the will of your Father who is in heaven that one of these little ones should perish" (Matthew 18:10).

God's Boundless Love for Every Soul

In this simple yet profound parable, Our Lord Jesus speaks of a shepherd who leaves behind ninety-nine sheep to search for the one that has gone astray on the mountainside. Throughout history, numerous artworks have depicted Our Lord Jesus Christ as a compassionate Good Shepherd, carrying a lost sheep over His shoulders while holding a staff.

The Parable of the Lost Sheep

This parable encapsulates the immense value God places on human souls. It is impossible to fully grasp the depth of God's love for everyone, a love that drives Him to pursue every soul. The divine liturgy according to Saint Gregory the theologian echoes this sentiment through the phrase, *"As a Good Shepherd, You have sought after that which had gone astray. As a true Father, You have laboured with me, the sick."* from the Liturgy according to Saint Gregory of Nazianzus, bishop of Constantinople. This phrase shows us the compassionate heart of Our Lord Jesus Christ

The parable serves as a guiding light, illuminating the profound love God holds for us. As we discussed earlier, a heart cannot be truly pure without being infused, impregnated, soaked and filled with God's love and the word of God. Consider the shepherd's actions: leaving ninety-nine sheep to find the one that strayed onto treacherous terrain. This sheep, driven by curiosity or stubbornness, abandoned the safety of the flock and the shepherd. Yet, the shepherd's concern for this lost sheep is unrelenting. "Why leave the ninety-nine?" one might ask. "You still have a vast majority. Why not let this one go?" But the shepherd cannot rest until the lost one is found. Such is the strength of Our Lord Jesus Christ's message. Such is the depth of His love, a love beyond measure.

Repentance: A Heavenly Celebration

The repeated emphasis on the joy in heaven over one repentant sinner, as highlighted by our Lord Jesus in both parables, underscores the paramount importance of repentance as the key to salvation. Saint Ephraim the Syrian beautifully expresses this idea, describing repentance as a feast for God. Repentance, in its transformative power, becomes an occasion of joy not only for the repentant soul but also for the heavenly hosts. The angels celebrate when repentance extends an invitation to them, creating a joyful banquet that resonates throughout the celestial realms.

The parable of the lost sheep provides a vivid and redemptive image of the process of bringing a lost sinner back to the path of truth. The sheep, having strayed from the flock, finds itself in perilous circumstances—deprived of sustenance and water, vulnerable to the threat of wild beasts. Similarly, a soul that has distanced itself from God, the source of truth and grace, faces various spiritual dangers, becoming an easy target for the adversary, as articulated in the Scriptures.

In the Lord's compassionate care for lost souls, a profound love is revealed. God's love for the world led Him to give His only begotten Son, ensuring that whoever believes in Him would not perish but have everlasting life (John 3:16). The sacrificial act of Christ on the Cross conquered death, and through His resurrection and Ascension, God continues to extend providential care for sinners. The Church, as the instrument of this divine care, persistently calls sinners to repentance, guiding them on the path of salvation.

Christ the Caring Shepherd

The imagery of the shepherd in the parable of the lost sheep is powerful and comforting. When the shepherd discovers the lost sheep, he does not drive it back to the flock forcefully. Instead, he compassionately takes it upon his shoulders, rejoicing, and bears it home. This parallels the journey of a repentant sinner who chooses to follow Christ. The initial steps of repentance may be challenging for the spiritually weakened individual, but the compassionate Shepherd-Christ, through His grace, strengthens and accompanies the repentant soul on the path of salvation. The sinner no longer walks alone; Christ, like the caring shepherd, lifts the burden, provides encouragement, and offers comfort. The invitation to "Come unto me, all ye who labour and are heavy laden, and I will give you rest" (Matthew 11:28) reflects the gentle and reassuring nature of Christ's guidance for those seeking repentance and salvation.

The Parable of the Lost Sheep

A Personal Encounter of Divine Pursuit for a Miraculous Conversion

A personal encounter underscores the mystery of this profound love: One Friday evening, Father Rafael asked me to lead the liturgy the following day on Saturday. He requested that I visit a sick man in the hospital and receives his blessings. This man, a widower living alone, had spent years rejecting God, the Church, and the sacraments. As I left the church that night, I crossed paths with Father Matthew. He saw that I seemed tired and exhausted and generously offered to lead the liturgy in my place, encouraging me to rest I was content with this arrangement, and the next morning, I remembered Father Matthew's suggestion. I wrestled with my decision, but a clear message from God compelled me to obey Father Rafael's request I attended the liturgy and later visited the hospital to see the gentleman.

I had never met this man before, and his demeanour was far from welcoming. He appeared uncomfortable and averted his gaze when I entered the room. His frailty made speech difficult, and my attempts at conversation were met with silence or indifference. I knelt by his bedside, offered prayers, and administered the absolution. I informed him of my intent to offer Holy Communion, but his reaction was unexpected. He opened his mouth as though to receive it, but suddenly he took the Host and threw it aside. Prompted by the Holy Spirit, I admonished him, my words unexpectedly stern, telling him that he had just spurned this last chance from God to repent and accept Him. I do not know what came over me; I even told him that his heart was as hard as a rock. But then tears welled in his eyes—a breakthrough. In that vulnerable moment, he began to open up. I guided him through confession, all the while tears of repentance mixing with his profound sorrow. He did not say much but would reply to my questions with gestures or a shake of the head. After granting him absolution, I offered Holy Communion again. His demeanour had transformed tranquillity and even a sense of angelic peace radiated from him. I congratulated him on the grace he had received and promised to return the next day. This encounter took place around 1Pm

Around 4 p.m. that same day, Father Rafael informed me that the man had passed away. We marvelled at how the Good Shepherd had sought out a lost sheep, even in his last moments, using His servants as vessels to bring His Body and Blood to the dying soul. I pondered the alternate outcome: What if I had decided to rest at home instead of leading the liturgy? What if I have decided to walk away after he spat the Holy Communion? What would have become of that soul? We play a small part, our movements orchestrated and inspired by God the Lover of mankind as we keep chanting in the midnight praise, serving His work and glory. This story, truly a work of God's grace, highlights His unending pursuit of the lost He does not desire the death of the sinner.

The Heart of the Good Shepherd

The core of this parable is Our Lord Jesus Christ's boundless love for creation and humanity. God desires every soul to return, embracing all, without exception. The message resonates with every heart—stubborn, wayward, hardened, or laden with thorns of sin. Can we hear the voice of the Good Shepherd? He weeps for us. Let us cry out to Him, seeking His protection. God's help is near, His love poured out through His blood, redeeming us. He labours unceasingly to save, refusing to see anyone lost the call is for every heart to turn to Him, surrendering fully. He lifts us up, carries us on His shoulders, and returns us to the fold. As St Luke's version of this parable states, *"I say to you that likewise there will be more joy in heaven over one sinner who repents than over ninety-nine just persons who need no repentance."* (Luke 15:7). However, obstinacy and distance from God will result in heartache. Beware, for a heart separated from God can be lost amidst the thorns of sin.

This is the Parable of the Shepherd, revealing Our Lord Jesus Christ's heart—a heart brimming with boundless love. Our deepest desire is to dissolve into His heart, evoking the joy that echoes through the heavens. Let sincere repentance flow from the core of our being, embracing God's unending love. Let us put away our excuses and jagged reasoning, for our stubbornness pales before the breadth of His love. Surrender, return, and experience the richness of His embrace. God's heart encompasses the entire world in its expansive love.

May today be the day we bring joy to those in heaven.

To You be the glory and honour, forever and ever. Amen.

Chapter 14

The Parable of the Slave and Forgiveness

"Then Peter came to Him and said, "Lord, how often shall my brother sin against me, and I forgive him? Up to seven times? "Our Lord Jesus said to him, "I do not say to you, up to seven times, but up to seventy times seven. Therefore the kingdom of heaven is like a certain king who wanted to settle accounts with his servants. And when he had begun to settle accounts, one was brought to him who owed him ten thousand talents. But as he was not able to pay, his master commanded that he be sold, with his wife and children and all that he had, and that payment be made. The servant therefore fell down before him, saying, 'Master, have patience with me, and I will pay you all.' Then the master of that servant was moved with compassion, released him, and forgave him the debt. "But that servant went out and found one of his fellow servants who owed him a hundred denarii; and he laid hands on him and took him by the throat, saying, 'Pay me what you owe!' So his fellow servant fell down at his feet and begged him, saying, 'Have patience with me, and I will pay you all.' And he would not, but went and threw him into prison till he should pay the debt. So when his fellow servants saw what had been done, they were very grieved, and came and told their master all that had been done. Then his master, after he had called him, said to him, 'You wicked servant! I forgave you all that debt because you begged me. Should you not also have had compassion on your fellow servant, just as I had pity on you?' And his master was angry, and delivered him to the torturers until he should pay all that was due to him. "So My heavenly Father also will do to you if each of you, from his heart, does not forgive his brother his trespasses." (Matthew 18:21-35).

Forgiveness as a Central Christian Virtue

In these verses, Our Lord Jesus imparts one of the most powerful lessons of forgiveness. Forgiving others is not merely a suggestion; it is an essential part of our spiritual journey. This parable about the unforgiving servant draws a sharp contrast between the enormous debt the servant owed his master and the small debt he refused to forgive in turn. The message is clear: God forgives us our immeasurable sins, and we should extend the same forgiveness to others. The essence of the parable teaches us to forgive our fellow servants who have sinned against us, especially if they fall down before us begging forgiveness. To interpret the parable in its particulars should be done only by one who has the mind of our Lord and Saviour Jesus Christ. Nevertheless, we shall attempt it. The kingdom is the Word of God, but it is not a kingdom of small extent, but of the heavens. The Word is likened to "a man who was a king", that is, He Who became incarnate for our sake and appeared in the likeness of men, and He settles accounts with His servants as a Good Judge. He does not punish without first judging: that would be cruel.

Speaking about forgiveness is not easy, as it can bring discomfort and stir up wounds that many wish to forget. Yet, the Bible's words on this topic are uncompromising. It is either black or white—forgive, and you will be forgiven; withhold forgiveness, and it will be withheld from you. These words might seem harsh, but they are a reminder of the role we play in the process. The key to forgiveness lies within us, regardless of the circumstances.

Abba Poimen the Hermit said this about Abba Isidore: "Whenever he addressed the brethren in church, he said only one thing: 'Forgive your brother, so that you, too, may be forgiven.'" That from the Sayings of the Desert Fathers.

The Obstacles to Forgiveness: Ego and Pride

The excuse of maintaining peace by not talking to someone often disguises the discord and hatred that resides within. This discord cannot foster genuine peace, and hatred cannot give birth to light. Love cannot be sown by the devil's hand. These excuses become an anaesthetic, numbing our conscience. To move forward, we must let go of these illusions.

Scripture offers profound guidance: *"Love will cover a multitude of sins"* (1 Peter 4:8). Love is our greatest asset in this world, the treasure we accumulate over a lifetime. These treasures of love are the drops of oil in our lamps, the essential ingredient for life's journey. Without love, life loses its flavour. Even the most remarkable acts, such as helping the poor or adorning churches, are meaningless without love. As Saint Paul says, *"Though I speak with the tongues of men and of angels, but have not love, I have become sounding brass or a clanging cymbal. And though I have the gift of prophecy, and understand all mysteries and all knowledge, and though I have all faith, so that I could remove mountains, but have not love, I am nothing."* (1 Corinthians 13:1-2*)*.

The Lord's forgiveness is heavenly grace, which, as we have already more than once emphasized, does not act automatically, but only with the indispensable participation of the believer. Of course, the King could, in a unilateral manner, forgive His servant, without his repentance; but He wants his debtor to learn from his magnanimous act and in his own life to act likewise.

Living in conflict with others means walking in darkness, not in light. *"But he who hates his brother is in darkness and walks in darkness, and does not know where he is going, because the darkness has blinded his eyes"* (1 John 2:11). To be a peacemaker, to sow peace instead of conflict, is to follow the path of light. It is we ourselves who owe ten thousand talents, receiving benefaction every day yet giving back nothing good to God in return. He who owes ten thousand talents is also that ruler who has received from God the protection and allegiance of many men, each man being like a talent, and then does not employ his sovereignty well. Selling the debtor along with his wife and children indicates alienation from God, for the one who is sold goes to another master. And is the wife not the flesh, being the mate of the soul, and the children, the evil deeds done by the soul and the body? He commands the flesh to be given to Satan for ravaging, that is, to be given over to illnesses or to the torment of the demons, but the children, that is to say, the doing of evil deeds, are given over to torture on the rack, as, for example, when God withers the hand that has stolen, or constricts it by means of a demon. See how the woman, which is the flesh, and the children, which is the doing of evil, have been given over to affliction so that the spirit might be saved, as in the case of that man who can no longer steal because his hand is crippled.

The Lord's teaching emphasizes the importance of forgiveness in the life of a believer. The passage from Matthew 5:23-24 *"Therefore if you bring your gift to the altar, and there remember that your brother has something against you, leave your gift there before the altar, and go your way. First be reconciled to your brother, and then come and offer your gift"* underscores that prayers offered to God are not accepted if the one praying harbours unforgiveness toward their neighbour. In this teaching, Jesus urges reconciliation before approaching the altar, emphasizing the significance of harmonious relationships with others in the worshipper's spiritual life.

The lesson conveyed is clear: forgiveness and reconciliation are integral aspects of Christian life. The ability to forgive, as taught by Jesus, extends beyond personal healing to the broader spiritual community. The parable underscores the interconnectedness of our actions and the awareness that our conduct has implications not only on an earthly level but also within the spiritual realm, prompting heavenly beings to observe and respond to acts of cruelty and forgiveness.

A symbolic story illustrates this concept: Two brothers shared a farm, living side by side in harmony. Discord arose due to a misunderstanding. The elder brother chanced upon a wandering carpenter, and he commissioned a wall to be built between their houses, a symbol of total separation. However, the wise carpenter understood the situation and built a bridge instead. The younger brother assumed it was the older brother who requested the bridge and came to greet him apologetically. This bridge became the catalyst for reconciliation, reminding the brothers of their shared love and bond. Realising what had happened, they invited the carpenter to stay with them, but he told them he could not, as he had many more bridges to build.

The call to be a peacemaker is the call to be a bridge builder like that carpenter. Not only will you be accomplishing God's will in people's lives, but your own relationships will grow richer, and you will draw closer to others.

Forgiving your brother is pivotal for salvation. The illusion that I can focus only on Christ while ignoring others violates the core principle of love. If I cannot love my visible brother, how can I claim to love an invisible God? *"If someone says, 'I love God,' and hates his brother, he is a liar; for he who does not love his brother whom he has seen, how can he love God whom he has not seen?"* (1 John 4:20).

We speak of forgiveness so much in the Church, so much in the Christian life, that, too often, we simply forget to listen. We forget the meaning of this term, of this idea, and this action, and we forget, too, the real centrality that it is to have in our life in Christ. It is a centrality that is nonetheless brought home time and time again, not only in the writings of the Fathers, but in the liturgical services of the Church, in the prayers, in the hymns, and in every corner and aspect of Orthodox life.

Without forgiveness, nothing. And yet, we lose track of forgiveness perhaps because we hear about it so often. Yet it remains key and central to all that we are and all that we do, and when we pay attention to what the Church says in her prayers and her hymns about the need to forgive, about the act of forgiving, tied in to the reality of receiving in our heart God's forgiveness, when we truly listen, we realize just how critical, just how central true forgiveness actually is.

This centrality is brought to mind by another saying of the Egyptian desert. Drawn from the Sayings of Abba Sisoes from the Apophthegmata, we have this.

Lessons from the Saints and Desert Fathers

A brother who was insulted by another brother came to the abba and said to him, "I was hurt, Abba, by my brother, and I wish to avenge myself."

The abba tried to console him, and he said, "Do not do this, my child. Rather, leave vengeance to God."

But he said, "I will not quit until I avenge myself."

Then the abba said, "Let us pray, brother." And, standing up, he proclaimed aloud, "Our Father, forgive us our trespasses just as we do not forgive those who trespass against us."

And hearing these words, the brother fell at the feet of the teacher and said, "I am not going to fight with my brother anymore. Forgive me, my dear father!"

Christian teaching always emphasizes the reciprocal nature of mercy, forgiveness, and love in the Christian life. It points to a common human tendency: while expecting and receiving various blessings from God, individuals may struggle to extend similar compassion to those seeking the same from them. The call to soften our hearts and show mercy aligns with the biblical teaching to forgive as we have been forgiven. It echoes Christ's commandment in (Luke 6:37): *"Judge not, and you shall not be judged. Condemn not, and you shall not be condemned. Forgive, and you will be forgiven.*

The parable illustrates the importance of reflecting God's mercy and forgiveness in our interactions with others. It serves as a reminder not to withhold the same grace that we have received from God. The call to soften our hearts suggests an ongoing process of self-examination and transformation, urging believers to recognize the benefactions received from God and extend similar kindness to others. In essence, the teaching encourages a spirit of generosity, compassion, and forgiveness in our relationships with fellow human beings—a living expression of the divine mercy we have experienced.

The love experienced by the Apostles transformed them from fishermen to fishers of men, is a testament to the power of love. Love grants strength, courage, and the ability to praise day and night. Love and forgiveness are gifts from God, bestowed upon those who fervently pray for them.

If we find ourselves avoiding others, blocking numbers, or harbouring grudges, it is time to humbly ask God for intervention. Deny our ego and let God work. Repeatedly ask Him, and we will witness divine intervention. God will orchestrate circumstances; perhaps leading the person we have avoided approaching us with an olive branch. Rejection of their approach out of pride is worse than the initial discord. Letting go of ego and pride is crucial for reconciliation.

Ego is the chief obstacle to forgiveness. All these points share a common thread—ego. One of our spiritual forefathers wished that God would crucify this ego, nailing it to the Cross. Let yourself feel the pain of these difficult situations and the part you have played in them, *"For godly sorrow produces repentance"* (2 Corinthians 7:10).

I would like to conclude this chapter with a beautiful story: There was a student attending a lecture given by His Holiness

The Parable of the Slave and Forgiveness

Pope Shenouda III at the Theological College in Cairo. This student stood in the middle of the lecture room and began to speak inappropriate words to His Holiness and insulting the Pope, accusing him of many things. The Pope lowered his face in guilt, admitting he had wronged and sinned against the student. The student continued to insult the Pope and attacked him. After enduring the abuse patiently, the Pope repeatedly replied, "Is there anything else my son"? The student could not take this any longer. The forgiveness, humility, love, long-suffering, and meekness were too much for him to bear. He collapsed in tears and wanted to kiss the feet of the Pope in apology. But the Pope took him, hugged him, and told him you are my son. The lesson this student learned in forgiveness was greater than any theological lesson he was attending.

I acknowledge that this topic is sensitive for many people, but if there is one thing to remember, it is the power of prayer for those who wrong us. Ask God to orchestrate the situation and trust Him to bring reconciliation.

To God be the glory and honour, forever and ever. Amen

Chapter 15

The Parable of the Eleventh Hour

"*For the kingdom of heaven is like a landowner who went out early in the morning to hire laborers for his vineyard. Now when he had agreed with the laborers for a denarius a day, he sent them into his vineyard. And he went out about the third hour and saw others standing idle in the marketplace, and said to them, 'You also go into the vineyard, and whatever is right I will give you.' So they went. Again he went out about the sixth and the ninth hour, and did likewise. And about the eleventh hour he went out and found others standing idle, and said to them, 'Why have you been standing here idle all day?' They said to him, 'Because no one hired us.' He said to them, 'You also go into the vineyard, and whatever is right you will receive.'* "So when evening had come, the owner of the vineyard said to his steward, 'Call the laborers and give them their wages, beginning with the last to the first' And when those came who were hired about the eleventh hour, they each received a denarius. But when the first came, they supposed that they would receive more; and they likewise received each a denarius. And when they had received it, they complained against the landowner, saying, 'These last men have worked only one hour, and you made them equal to us who have

The Parable of the Eleventh Hour

borne the burden and the heat of the day.' But he answered one of them and said, 'Friend, I am doing you no wrong. Did you not agree with me for a denarius? Take what is yours and go your way. I wish to give to this last man the same as to you. Is it not lawful for me to do what I wish with my own things? Or is your eye evil because I am good?' So the last will be first, and the first last For many are called, but few chosen." (Matthew 20:1-16).

Understanding the Kingdom of Heaven

This parable illustrates a key concept of the Kingdom of Heaven. Our Lord Christ' teachings consistently revolve around the Kingdom of heaven, and understanding its principles can significantly transform our lives. By focusing on Jerusalem, Golgotha, and salvation, like Our Lord Jesus did, we align ourselves with the core message of the Gospel.

The parable delves into four fundamental aspects:

1. The Heart of Our Lord
2. The Weighing Scale of Our Lord
3. The Accounts of Our Lord
4. People's opinions that sometimes affects us

In this parable, labourers are hired at various times throughout the day. Those who worked only an hour received the same wage as those who worked the entire day.

The Lord's Weighing Scale

Let us delve into the weighing scale of the Lord's perspective. His scale is profoundly just and perceptive. His accounts operate differently from the world's standards. In today's context, if such an occurrence unfolded in a company, it would likely cause outrage and claims of injustice. But God's divine accounts transcend our understanding. His insights are hidden from our human perspective.

Why does the Lord operate this way?

God's vision encompasses more than we can see. His compassionate eyes discern beyond the surface. It is an expression of tenderness toward those who entered the vineyard at the eleventh hour. Many of us find ourselves standing with them. God sees the hardships faced by people—innocent children oppressed by circumstances, individuals whose dreams were crushed by life's challenges, and those who turn to God later in life. God perceives a young boy burdened by situations beyond his control, a woman whose aspirations were curtailed by her chaotic home environment, a young man shifting his focus to eternal matters but frequently stumbling, individuals whose lives were marred by negative environments, young souls whose dreams were shattered by family issues, people drawn into wrong company due to parental neglect, and those whose church experiences were tainted by negative interactions.

A Message of Hope and Second Chances

God looks at these individuals and acknowledges that obstacles hindered their spiritual growth. He sees the eleventh-hour workers, and He extends them another opportunity, a second chance. Many of us relate to these situations and stand alongside them.

The parable challenges any notion of entitlement based on external factors, such as being the first members of God's Kingdom. Instead, it highlights the importance of sincerity, diligence, pure love, and humility in God's evaluation of human works. The example of the good thief on the cross is presented as a powerful illustration of this principle, emphasizing the immediate and sincere repentance that granted him access to the Kingdom of Heaven.

Saint John Chrysostom adds an excellent supplement to this parable of the Lord: *"If any be pious and God-loving, let him enjoy this fair and radiant solemnity. If any be a wise servant, let him enter rejoicing into the joy of his Lord. If any have laboured in fasting, let him receive now his denarius. If any have wrought from the first hour, let him receive today his just due. If any have come after the third hour, let him feast with thankfulness. If any have arrived after the sixth hour, let him doubt nothing, for he will in no way suffer loss. If any have come later than even the ninth hour, let him draw nigh, doubting nothing, fearing nothing."*

Beloved reader, today God invites us to forgive the past and embrace a second chance. He has countless tasks for us. This parable is referenced – "Count me among those of the eleventh hour" – in the Eleventh Hour prayer of the book of Agpeya; a message of hope and renewed opportunities. Many thousands have entered the Kingdom through this door of second chances. God desires us to work for these souls—to provide a second chance, to extend a helping hand, and to lend a listening ear. There are countless opportunities to guide those who are lost, to support those who are oppressed, and to uplift those who are broken.

Our Role in God's Work

Our Coptic Orthodox Church includes this reading in the Eleventh Hour prayer for a reason. This hour symbolizes hope, renewal, and a fresh start. God wants us to be part of His work—to be instruments of His love, to lift the fallen, to heal the broken-hearted, to encourage the discouraged, and to inspire the hopeless. God has many houses in Heaven, yet they are not yet filled. He has numerous souls who long for His mercy, many lives in need of our compassion.

"Many are called." God is inviting us to work side by side with Him. Together, we can uplift, support, and encourage those who need a second chance. Consider our own lives—how we, too, were once eleventh-hour workers, given a fresh opportunity. God invites us to participate in His divine work, to extend His grace, and to bring many more souls into His Kingdom.

The concluding exhortation to " Enter into the joy of your Lord " and the vivid imagery of people from various backgrounds, rich and poor, abstemious, and slothful, all celebrating together, conveys a message of unity and shared joy in God's abundant grace. The call to "receive all ye the wealth of goodness" echoes the theme of a generous and all-encompassing divine mercy.

The Power of Faithfulness

Finally, what about people's opinions that sometimes affects us? This is a tremendous parable which illustrates an important truth: It is not the amount of time which you serve or the prominence or importance of your position which determines your reward. Rather, you will be rewarded for your faithfulness to the task which God has given you to perform, regardless of how insignificant it appears or the length of time you serve. However, only God is able to judge your faithfulness, therefore, do not watch what others are doing and do not become distracted by what they say about you, but be faithful to do what God has called you to do. *"So the last shall be first, and the first last."*

The insight provided emphasizes the fundamental distinction between worldly standards of greatness and God's criteria for evaluating one's worthiness of heavenly rewards. It underscores the idea that human judgment and recognition often based on worldly achievements and prominence may not necessarily align with God's assessment of an individual's faithfulness in serving Him.

The notion that heavenly rewards are not merely a result of working for them but are bestowed in response to faithful service aligns with the biblical understanding of God's grace and justice. The emphasis is on the authenticity and sincerity of one's service to God, rather than a transactional approach where rewards are earned as a payment for works.

This perspective reflects the biblical teachings that highlight the importance of motives, intentions, and the condition of the heart in God's assessment of human actions. It resonates with passages such as (Matthew 6:1-4), where our Lord Jesus emphasizes the sincerity of giving to the needy without seeking recognition from others.

Conclusion

In summary, the insight provided serves as a valuable reminder that the pursuit of heavenly rewards is not about working for personal gain but about faithfully responding to God's call and serving with a sincere heart. It redirects the focus from worldly standards of greatness to a more profound understanding of God's grace and the transformative power of a faithful life. To God be the glory and honour, forever and ever. Amen.

Chapter 16

The Parable of the Two Sons

"But what do you think? A man had two sons, and he came to the first and said, 'Son, go, work today in my vineyard.' He answered and said, 'I will not,' but afterward he regretted it and went. Then he came to the second and said likewise. And he answered and said, 'I go, sir,' but he did not go. Which of the two did the will of his father?" They said to Him, "The first" Our Lord Jesus said to them, "Assuredly, I say to you that tax collectors and harlots enter the kingdom of God before you. For John came to you in the way of righteousness, and you did not believe him; but tax collectors and harlots believed him; and when you saw it, you did not afterward relent and believe him." (Matthew 21:28-32).

The Lesson for the Pharisees

Our Lord Jesus spoke this simple parable to the stubborn elders and Pharisees, who resisted Our Lord Jesus Christ, even during the time of John the Baptist Our Lord Jesus Christ, told them that John came in the way of righteousness, and you did not believe him. This was always the problem with the hypocritical Pharisees, wearing fig leaves to cover their cheating and nakedness, not wanting to live the truth and the way of righteousness.

A true Christian lives with our Lord Jesus Christ according to His commandments, according to His words and His Holy Spirit, walks in the way of righteousness, because Our Lord Jesus is the truth. Our Lord Jesus said to them that John came in the way of righteousness, but you did not believe him and did not change.

The Two Sons: Two Types of People

Interestingly we notice in this parable the first son was praised twice; once for his honesty for not giving a promise that he would not keep and the second time when he retracted his sin and went back to carry out his father's will. The second son slandered twice, once when he promised but did not fulfil and the second time by disobeying his father's will.

This shows us that there are two types of people: those who obey and fulfil the promise and those who are stubborn and defensive, like the Pharisees. Our Lord Jesus Christ said, *"Not everyone who says to Me, 'Lord, Lord,' shall enter the kingdom of heaven, but he who does the will of My Father in heaven."* (Matthew 7:21). Here, the Lord asks both to work in the vineyard (the Church). The first type represents the Gentiles who began their life refusing, then came back in repentance and worked with Our Lord Jesus. The second type represents the Jews who said, *"here I am master,"* but did nothing. That is how they lost the privilege of the vineyard. The first type represents the tax collectors and the sinners who left God at the beginning of their life, then repented and returned to God at the end. The second type represents the superficial Our Lord Jesus Christian person, who fulfils all their formal obligations and who is seen worshipping God, but they do not do His will in their life. The Bible says about this type of person, *"Having a form of godliness but denying its power." (2 Timothy 3:5).* Those places will be taken away from them to be given to the repented sinners.

Repentance and a New Heart

Why does God name harlots in this parable? It is certainly an abominable sin in God's eyes, *"You shall not commit adultery" (Exodus 20:14); "Flee sexual immorality. Every sin that a man does is outside the body, but he who commits sexual immorality sins against his own body" (1 Corinthians 6:18); "You have a few names even in Sardis who have not defiled their garments" (Revelation 3:4); "And you have polluted the land with your harlotries and your wickedness" (Jeremiah 3:2).* So, it seems strange that the Lord said that these harlots will be ahead of us in the kingdom of heaven. God is showing us how wide the window opens for repentance and hope.

One day Abba Serapion passed through an Egyptian village and there he saw a courtesan who stayed in her own cell. The old man said to her, 'Expect me this evening, for I should like to come and spend the night with you.' She replied, 'Very well, abba.' She got ready and made the bed. When evening came, the old man came to see her and entered her cell and said to her, 'Have you got the bed ready?' She said, 'Yes, Abba.' Then he closed the door and said to her, 'Wait a bit, for we have a rule of prayer, and I must fulfil that first. So, the old man began his prayers. He took the Psalter and at each psalm he said a prayer for the courtesan, begging God that she might be converted and saved, and God heard him.

The woman stood trembling and praying beside the old man. When he had completed the whole Psalter, the woman fell to the ground. Then the old man, beginning the Epistle, read a great deal from the apostle and completed his prayers. The woman was filled with compunction and understood that he had not come to see her to commit sin but to save her soul and she fell at his feet, saying, 'Abba, do me this kindness and take me where I can please God.' So, the old man took her to a monastery of virgins and entrusted her to the Amma and he said, 'Take this sister and do not put any yoke or commandment on her as on the other sisters, but if she wants something, give it to her and allow her to walk as she wishes.' After some days, the courtesan said, 'I am a sinner; I wish to eat every second day.' A little later she said, 'I have committed many sins, and I wish to eat every fourth day.' A few days later she besought the Amma saying, 'Since I have grieved God greatly by my sins, do me the kindness of putting me in a cell and shutting it completely and giving me a little bread and some work through the window.' The Amma did so and the woman pleased God all the rest of her life.

The late Father Bishoy Kamel said that adulterers have a great power of love, which, when they return to the Lord, they come with all their heart. God wants the heart, not merely the obligatory works of those who say "yes," but do not do His will. He wants us to live with Him with all our hearts. He wants us to do everything with all our hearts; when we pray, when we are joyful, when we serve, when we read the Bible, and when we give money to the poor, we do it with all our love and from the depth of our heart. When we deal with others in this way, we enter the kingdom of God in our heart as Our Lord Jesus Christ describes in Luke 17:21, *"The kingdom of God is within you"*.

A Call to Give God Your Heart

The following is one of the most beautiful stories of repentance told by the late Father Youssef Asaad: He knew of a woman who was an adulterer and opened her house for men in exchange for money. He prayed much for her and her salvation and placed her name on the altar, until he felt God guiding him to go. He knocked on her door. She opened the door and asked him who he was. He replied, "A person begging for the mercy of God." She laughed sarcastically and invited him in. When he entered, he found the place filled with alcohol, cigarettes and cards and she was very scantily dressed. The Holy Spirit worked in him and placed the words in his mouth saying that we need God at all times. He spoke for two hours. During this time, she was drinking and smoking, but did not utter a word. Finally, she said to him, "Your words are good; come again." He asked her if he could pray for her. She did not object, so he prayed for God's mercy, for He loves the sinner and opens His arms to all those who repent. He went a second time. She was in the same condition as the first time. He continued to repeat his visits to her, until one day he found she was dressed more decently. He was incredibly happy, as this is the first step of the thousand miles on the road to repentance and reconciliation with God. She began to repent and confess all her past sins. The father saw all the changes that happened in her life because of her repentance. How beautiful were the stories of her repentance which gave comfort to the priest she told him that she had a block of units which she purchased with the money of sin and sold it. She wanted to know what she should do with this money. He said throw it in the river. He told her that God wants her heart, not her money. One day she asked him to take her to church and as they passed over a bridge, she opened a bag filled with money, which she threw out into the water. As she entered the church, she kissed the ground. Eventually, when she passed away, Father Youssef Assad attended her funeral. When he bent down to kiss her coffin, he smelt a beautiful aroma coming from it. How great the repentance of a sinner and how far ahead of us will they be ahead in the kingdom of heaven.

A Call to Give God Your Heart

God has called us today, saying, *"My son, give Me your heart"* (Proverbs 23:26), and I will change it completely; *"I will give you a new heart and put a new spirit within you"*

(Ezekiel 36:26), in order to change you all into saints.

To You is the glory and the honour, forever and ever. Amen.

Chapter 17

The Parable of the Wicked Vinedressers

"Hear another parable: There was a certain landowner who planted a vineyard and set a hedge around it, dug a winepress in it and built a tower. And he leased it to vinedressers and went into a far country. Now when vintage-time drew near, he sent his servants to the vinedressers, that they might receive its fruit. And the vinedressers took his servants, beat one, killed one, and stoned another. Again he sent other servants, more than the first, and they did likewise to them. Then last of all he sent his son to them, saying, 'They will respect my son.' But when the vinedressers saw the son, they said among themselves, 'This is the heir. Come, let us kill him and seize his inheritance.' So they took him and cast him out of the vineyard and killed him. "Therefore, when the owner of the vineyard comes, what will he do to those vinedressers?" They said to Him, "He will destroy those wicked men miserably, and lease his vineyard to other vinedressers who will render to him the fruits in their seasons." Our Lord Jesus said to them, "Have you never read in the Scriptures: 'The stone which the builders rejected Has become the chief cornerstone. This was the LORD's doing, and it is marvellous in our eyes'? "Therefore I say to you, the kingdom of God *will be taken from you and given to a nation bearing the fruits of it. And whoever falls on this stone will be broken; but on whomever it falls, it will grind him to powder." Now when the chief priests and Pharisees heard His parables, they perceived that He was speaking of them. But when they sought to lay hands on Him, they feared the multitudes, because they took Him for a prophet."* (Matthew 21:33-44).

This parable holds significant symbolism, portraying the Jewish nation's response to the arrival of Jesus Christ the landowner symbolises God the Father, while the vineyard represents us, His people, encompassed by a protective hedge representing His commandments and teachings. The landowner's journey to a far country suggests entrusting us with His creation and blessings, demonstrating God's trust in us.

The question emerges: Who is the true owner? It is not us; it is God. Our possessions, talents, resources—everything is entrusted to us by God. The parable teaches humility and accountability. Our role is to be faithful stewards and yield spiritual fruits for God. These fruits bring joy, just as grapes yield wine—a symbol of joy. Our lives should be a joyful testimony of God's grace.

The parable underscores God's expectation of receiving fruits from His vineyard—our lives. The Bible, Agpeya prayers, commemorating the saints and our services all remind us repeatedly of our purpose, and that at any moment we might face God's accountability.

Consider the vinedressers of the parable. Through their actions they tell God, "You'll get nothing from us!" thinking how they might reap the rewards for themselves. This is akin to rejecting God's rightful ownership over our lives. It reflects a rebellious attitude—the inclination to live life independently, separate from God's guidance. It shows the depths of our ignorance and our ingratitude, forgetting all that the Lord has done for us. Imagine the audacity of a child telling their parent, "You have done nothing for me, so I'll take everything and live life the way I want to." Yet how often do we say this to God? This attitude manifests when we ignore God's Word, neglect prayer, and prioritise our desires over His will.

Suppose that one day I go bankrupt, and a rich benefactor comes along and offers me a high-earning job with a large sign-on bonus that will cover all my expenses. When they call in to check on my work, I say, "sorry, I've got nothing for you." "You'll get nothing from us" is unjust and ungrateful. It qualified the vinedressers to be called "wicked." I should be extremely careful not to make the same qualification.

Do we serve God diligently or neglect His rights over our lives? The parable offers two distinct paths: being a faithful servant or a wicked one. Our lives will either leave a transformative legacy on the people we meet, or we will leave having made truly slight difference, burying our talents and keeping God's gifts for ourselves. Consider your own life: how many hundreds or thousands of people have you met whose name you hardly remember, and whose impact was completely forgettable? Now think of that small handful of people who have had the most profound impact on your life; possibly transforming it completely. This is the choice God places before us in this parable.

This parable underscores the importance of recognising God's ownership, fulfilling our roles as diligent stewards, and offering the fruits of a purposeful life. It is a call to choose to stand alongside the faithful servants who honour God's ownership and live with accountability, rather than among the wicked who deny His rights over their lives.

To God be the glory and honour, forever and ever. Amen.

Chapter 18

The Parable of the Wedding Feast - Part 1

"*And Our Lord Jesus answered and spoke to them again by parables and said: "The kingdom of heaven is like a certain king who arranged a marriage for his son, and sent out his servants to call those who were invited to the wedding; and they were not willing to come. Again, he sent out other servants, saying, 'Tell those who are invited, "See, I have prepared my dinner; my oxen and fatted cattle are killed, and all things are ready. Come to the wedding." But they made light of it and went their ways, one to his own farm, another to his business. And the rest seized his servants, treated them spitefully, and killed them. But when the king heard about it, he was furious. And he sent out his armies, destroyed those murderers, and burned up their city. Then he said to his servants, The wedding is ready, but those who were invited were not worthy. Therefore go into the highways, and as many as you find, invite to the wedding. So those servants went out into the highways and gathered together all whom they found, both bad and good. And the wedding hall was filled with guests. "But when the king came in to see the guests, he saw a man there who did not have on a wedding garment. So he said to him, 'Friend, how did you come in here without a wedding garment?' And he was speechless. Then the king said to the servants, 'Bind him hand and foot, take him away, and cast him into outer darkness; there will be weeping and gnashing of teeth.' "For many are called, but few are chosen."* (Matthew 22:1-14).

The Invitation to the Kingdom

In this parable, we encounter the third narrative related to the invitation to enter His kingdom. The first story portrayed two sons—one who heeded the call and the other who did not. The second narrative unveiled the actions of the wicked servants.

Now, we come to the poignant parable that concludes Our Lord Jesus' teachings beginning with, "The kingdom of heaven is like…" This story paints a beautiful picture of a king orchestrating a wedding for his son. It is a narrative filled with intricate details that hold a profound message for us. The king meticulously prepares a grand feast and sends out numerous invitations, beckoning people to join the wedding celebration.

Typically, when attending such events, we act as spectators. However, in this instance, the invitees are not just observers. They are personally invited to actually be the groom and the bride. As mentioned in 2 Corinthians 11:2, *"For I have betrothed you to one husband, that I may present you as a chaste virgin to Our Lord Jesus Christ"* Thus, this invitation is not merely for an audience; it is an intimate call for the human soul, depicted as *"a bride adorned for her husband"* (Revelation 21:2).

A Warning with a Sharper Edge

These three parables were taught toward the conclusion of Our Lord Jesus Christ's life; around the time He entered the temple to cleanse it. Consequently, the tone bears a sharper edge, underscoring the consequences of disregarding the Teacher's instructions—resulting in *"weeping and gnashing of teeth."*

In this story, God extends the invitation to many for the grand celebration—*"In My Father's house are many mansions"* (John 14:2), and *"Who desires all men to be saved and to come to the knowledge of the truth"* (1 Timothy 2:4). His intention is for all to be saved, thus the instruction in the parable to summon everyone.

Pause for a moment to ponder the responses of those invited. *"They made light of it and went their ways."* Imagine the proud parent who spares no expense to organise a wedding reception and invites many and has no one arrive. Yet this is not unheard of in our world today.

The Distractions of Life

Consider where the people who declined the king's invitation went to their farms and to their businesses. It is realistic that *everyone* would have had such urgent matters to attend to? Our Lord Jesus Christ very strongly implies that they could have attended the wedding if they really wanted to, yet decided to distract themselves with work that they could convince themselves was 'important.' Similarly, we are summoned by God during prayer times. Our Lord Jesus Christ eagerly desires communion with us during these quiet moments. He yearns to speak with us as a father to his child. Yet, we offer countless excuses—busy with our emails, our errands, a few minutes of work on our laptop that rolls into a few hours, or sometimes just wanting to finish off a TV series.

It is alarming how many people these days seem reluctant to engage in prayer. The conscience, it appears, no longer pricks. Prayerlessness has become the norm. In times past, this would have been seen as peculiar. But today, despite prayer being the gateway to the kingdom and the throne of grace—*"Let us therefore come boldly to the throne of grace, that we may obtain mercy and find grace to help in time of need"* (Hebrews 4:16)—many are apathetic.

The Power of Prayer

How can we triumph over the devil if we shun standing before Our Lord Jesus Christ in prayer? How can we safeguard our homes, lives, marriages, children, and grandchildren from evil without lifting our hands in prayer? How can our dwellings brim with joy and peace without inviting the groom and the owner of the house? How can we intercede for those enduring adversity if we fail to pray and implore God's intervention? How can individuals transform if we do not petition the Lord's intervention? How can anyone change without earnestly seeking God's guidance?

Years back, I approached my confession Father with a problem I was experiencing. His response remains engraved in my memory: "Go to your room, shut the door, and squeeze yourself before the Lord." It was my first encounter with the expression, 'squeeze yourself'?

This is how to pray effectively. Do not hold on to any of your fears or problems but squeeze every last drop of anxiety and worry before God.

A Hidden Treasure in the Parable

In my humble perspective, there is a concealed treasure within this parable, much like all the parables shared by our Lord Our Lord Jesus. Parables frequently convey profound spiritual and moral teachings. The invitation to the wedding feast serves as a personal and intimate summons to the human soul, emphasizing the profound connection between God and

His children. This parable vividly underscores the significance of responding to this invitation with genuine sincerity and unwavering dedication

Chapter 19

The Parable of the Wedding Feast - Part 2

"A certain man gave a great supper and invited many, and sent his servant at supper time to say to those who were invited, 'Come, for all things are now ready. But they all with one accord began to make excuses. The first said to him, 'I have bought a piece of ground, and I must go and see it. I ask you to have me excused.' And another said, 'I have bought five yoke of oxen, and I am going to test them. I ask you to have me excused.'' Still another said, 'I have married a wife, and therefore I cannot come.' So that servant came and reported these things to his master. Then the master of the house, being angry, said to his servant, 'Go out quickly into the streets and lanes of the city, and bring in here the poor and the maimed and the lame and the blind.' And the servant said, 'Master, it is done as you commanded, and still there is room.' Then the master said to the servant, 'Go out into the highways and hedges, and compel them to come in, that my house may be filled. For I say to you that none of those men who were invited shall taste my supper.'" (Luke 14:15-24)

The Parable of the Wedding Feast (2)

The Significance of the Invitation

This parable is the parallel telling of last chapter's Parable of the Wedding Feast from Matthew 22, with a few differences that we can extract spiritual gems from.

The first verse tells us that the servant was delivering the invitations towards the evening – supper time. Yet, consider the excuses. Is it realistic for someone to test an ox in the dark? It clearly seems like an excuse, indicating a lack of necessity for God in his life. This portrays that God is non-essential to him and that material wealth and worldly possessions hold greater importance. Instead of attending the king's son's wedding feast, his priorities lay with his oxen and possessions. This notion aligns with Revelation 3:17, *"Because you say, 'I am rich, have become wealthy, and have need of nothing'—and do not know that you are wretched, miserable, poor, blind, and naked."* This desperate lack is of God's righteousness, which is why the next verse continues to say *"I counsel you to buy from Me gold refined in the fire, that you may be rich; and white garments, that you may be clothed, that the shame of your nakedness may not be revealed."*

The Distractions of Worldly Concerns

Continuing with the parable, the next person offered an excuse, stating, *"I have married a wife, and therefore I cannot come."* This individual is preoccupied with his spouse, his family, his finances, his children's academic success, and numerous other worldly concerns, leaving no space for God. While it is necessary and commendable to attend to family matters, the question remains—where does Our Lord Jesus stand in his life? Where is Christ's faith he should be passing on, just as it was passed down by parents, grandparents, Sunday school servants, deacons, and church fathers? What legacy is he leaving for his children? Is it just knowledge and worldly provisions, or is it a life imbued with faith? Does he tell them about our Lord Jesus Christ? Do they witness and see the Lord Christ within him? There is a world of difference between telling one's children about the power and importance of prayer and them witnessing their parent kneeling in private, fervently praying over life's challenges. Do we go around texting and posting Bible verses and sermon links, or do we strive to be a living Bible—a testament to practicing and living what it teaches?

The Host's Anger and God's call

How did the host of the banquet respond to these excuses? The scripture says, *"He was furious."* This parable describes how our heavenly Father feels when we disregard Our Lord Jesus Christ's call for eternal life, be it through lack of prayer or repentance. It is one of the rare instances in which the emotions of our Lord are revealed when we neglect Him. The parable commences with joy, for the Kingdom of Heaven is synonymous with jubilation—a banquet prepared, a wedding celebration. Yet, it concludes with wrath. After all, was not he preparing for this grand occasion?

The Meaning of "All Things Are Now Ready"

In verse 17, we encounter the phrase, *"All things are now ready."* Often, these words are overlooked unintentionally. What encompasses "all things"? They encompass the Incarnation, Our Lord Jesus Christ's self-abasement, His willingness to be crucified, the agony, the scourging, the humiliation, the resurrection, salvation, the establishment of the Church, the Holy Communion, the bestowal of the Holy Spirit, and the sacraments. These elements collectively constitute the "all things" referred to.

The parable describes that all the guests, *"with one accord,"* proffer excuses. This scenario mirrors the present world—many of us engage in this practice. However, we are not guiltless just because everyone around us does the same thing. As Saint Augustine says: "Wrong is wrong, even if everyone is doing it. Right is right, even if no one does it."

he parable advances, as the host directs his servants to invite people from the highways, streets, and lanes. While overseeing the guests, he identifies a man not adorned in a wedding garment. In those times, hosts would provide clothing for the attendees. This raises the question—what are these wedding garments? They symbolize baptism, grace, righteousness, and, most importantly, being clothed in Our Lord Jesus. *"But put on the Lord Our Lord Jesus Our Lord Jesus Christ"* (Romans 13:14).

To put on our Lord Jesus Christ implies immersion in Him, becoming hidden within Him, united with Him, abiding in Him and dying in Him. God's righteousness envelops us, grace shrouds us. Our actions, interactions, and utterances are enveloped in Our Lord Jesus Christ, as though Our Lord Jesus Christ Himself were the doer or speaker. It might seem impossible, yet it is God, Our Lord Jesus Christ, and the Holy Spirit working within us, *"He must increase, but I must decrease"* (John 3:30).

A Living Example of Faith

Beloved brethren, we are thankful for the living examples among us, embodying Our Lord Jesus Christ's presence. Let me share the story of an extraordinary story about an extraordinary lady who dwelt among us. While we knew her, she remained unaware of her preciousness in the eyes of the Lord and God's righteousness that bestowed and covered her during her final years. God granted us the privilege and the blessing of witnessing her journey through a formidable disease. She endured this trial for four and a half years, shouldering her cross with contentment, joy, patience, tolerance, purity, and a steadfast spirit. She was an unassuming woman, a devoted wife and mother, adorned with a unique grace, housed within a pure heart. She never succumbed to anger, judgment, conflict, or gossip. Her life centred on fostering peace, serving others, and kindling happiness in their lives. In her last months, her pain was excruciating and unendurable. Nevertheless, she embraced her tribulation and accepted an unfavourable prognosis without a hint of complaint. Though the burden was weighty, she never lamented, nor did she ask, "Why me?" or "What about my young children left behind?"

The Invitation to The Heavenly Wedding

Allow me to recount her last moments on earth. As we stood by her around the bed, she suddenly gestured waving her hands at us to be silent. When asked why, she responded, "I can hear something very important—it sounds like an announcement. I've received an invitation to a wedding, a heavenly wedding." We began to pray the Sunset Prayer from the book of Agpeya. After we read the Gospel and when we reached the third litany, where we implore, *"Our Lady Virgin Mary, guide me to the means of repentance, to you I plea, through you I seek supplication, I call you for help, lest I fail. Come to my rescue, when my soul departs from my body, defeat the conspiracies of the enemy,"* at that particular moment, her soul departed. She embarked on her journey, prepared to relish the heavenly wedding feast and partake in the supper of the King's Son.

May God bestow upon us the wisdom to put away our excuses that we may join her and the host of Our Lord Jesus Christ's faithful who have come before us at the supper of the king's son.

Yours is the glory and honour, forever and ever, Amen.

Chapter 20

The Parable of the Fig Tree
- Part 1

"Now learn this parable from the fig tree: When its branch has already become tender and puts forth leaves, you know that summer is near. So you also, when you see all these things, know that it is near—at the doors! Assuredly, I say to you, this generation will by no means pass away till all these things take place. Heaven and earth will pass away, but My words will by no means pass away" (Matthew 24:32-35).

This brief parable, though consisting of only a few lines, conveys the profound teachings of Our Lord Jesus Christ about the Kingdom of Heaven and the path to eternal life. Through it, Our Lord seeks to illuminate the realities of heaven and prepare our hearts to enter it. He calls us to lift our gaze beyond the distractions of this world and secure a place within the heavenly embrace. My earnest desire and constant prayer are that our Lord will plant the remembrance of heaven deep within our thoughts, minds, eyes, and hearts, guiding us continually toward His eternal kingdom.

Keep Infusing the Aroma of the Kingdom

How wonderful it would be to infuse these heavenly thoughts into our children and those around us! Let us sow these seeds as Our Lord Jesus Christ did, nurturing them with the love of God. Through His grace, fortified by His salvation, His precious blood, and His redemption, we shall unite in heaven, bound together by eternal life, hand in hand. Imagine the splendour of such an existence—an intimate, unbroken communion with God. As Our Lord Jesus said, *"Father, I desire that they also whom You gave Me may be with Me"* (John 17:24), and *"I go to prepare a place for you, that where I am, there you may be also"* (John 14:2-3). He assures us, *"Those whom You gave Me I have kept; and none of them is lost"* (John 17:12). This is the promise of a life everlasting in His presence—a divine unity and joy that surpasses all.

Within this parable, Our Lord Jesus alludes to His Second Coming. His disciples had asked, *"Tell us, when will these things be? And what will be the sign of Your coming...?"* (Matthew 24:3). He listed for them a number of signs and portents that would precede the last days, and then He directed their attention to the fig tree, whose branches and leaves heralded the approaching summer. Similarly, our life with Our Lord Jesus Christ is marked by such indicators, signifying His nearness. Consequently, He urges us to prepare ourselves, poised for the wedding day.

Dear beloved, act wisely, for the days are fraught with malevolence. *"Redeeming the time, because the days are evil. Therefore, do not be unwise, but understand what the will of the Lord is"* (Ephesians 5:16-17). Thus, what must we do? This query will be addressed through parables that we shall explore later.

Preparing for the Kingdom

As we journey through life, we must keep this truth ever before us:

- **Cement this notion within our minds, hearts, and gaze.** Let the promise of the Kingdom be our constant focus.
- **Embrace this principle, fixing our sight on it.** Hold tightly to the vision of heaven, allowing it to guide your every step.
- **Transmit it to our children, loved ones, and all around us** by continually planting the seeds of the Kingdom. Speak of God's promises, live them out, and let others see heaven reflected in your life. Let me share with you the best way you teach this to your kids, by modelling, modelling, and modelling,
- **Wait on the Lord with good courage and good cheer, persevering through the trials of earthly existence.** Keep faith, trusting in God's perfect timing and His unending love as you press on toward the eternal joy that awaits.

Through these simple yet profound actions, we prepare not only ourselves but also those we love for the Kingdom of Heaven, holding fast to the hope of eternal life with God.

The Importance of Preparedness

Why do I emphasize preparedness? Throughout the teachings of Our Lord Jesus Christ and the Church's instructions, we frequently encounter the directive to be ready. This call is not merely a suggestion but a vital aspect of our spiritual journey. While some may find these words daunting, they carry immense significance.

In our contemporary world, these themes of readiness and vigilance have often faded from everyday conversations, replaced by new doctrines or dismissed as discouraging. However, for the Church and her servants, these teachings remain essential. They are not just theological ideas but a profound embodiment of our relationship with God, urging us to live in a state of constant spiritual awareness.

This emphasis on preparedness is not meant to advocate for a life of perpetual sorrow or lamentation. On the contrary, the call to readiness is intertwined with the joy of the Gospel. If we fail to convey the joy inherent in eternal life, then we have missed the heart of the message. Preparedness should fill us with hope and anticipation, reminding us that our ultimate destination is heaven, where true joy and peace dwell forever.

Voices Calling Us to the Truth

Throughout the Bible, we encounter voices boldly proclaiming the truth, urging us to turn our hearts towards God and heaven. In the days of Noah, sceptics were plentiful, yet he remained steadfast in his message. Prophets like Jeremiah, Isaiah, Ezekiel, and Joel raised their voices to sound alarms among a hardened populace, calling them back to God.

John the Baptist famously preached, *"Repent, for the kingdom of heaven is at hand!"* (Matthew 3:2). His message was a wake-up call, emphasizing the urgency of spiritual readiness. The Apostle Paul also echoed these sentiments, reminding us of our true citizenship: *"For our citizenship is in heaven, from which we also eagerly wait for the Saviour"* (Philippians 3:20). He encouraged believers by saying, *"For our light affliction, which is but for a moment, is working for us a far more exceeding and eternal weight of glory"* (2 Corinthians 4:17). Paul's teachings consistently revolved around the splendour of heaven, highlighting that earthly suffering pales in comparison to the glory awaiting us: *"For I consider that the sufferings of this present time are not worthy to be compared with the glory which shall be revealed in us"* (Romans 8:18). His longing was clear when he expressed, *"I* have a desire to depart and be with Our Lord Jesus Christ, which is far better"* (Philippians 1:23).

Preparing for the Heavenly Wedding: A Reflection

Allow me to conclude with a narrative from our cherished mentor, Father Tadros Yacoub Malaty a prolific writer and theologian based at the famous church of Saint George in Sporting, Alexandra: This account unfolds in one of the countries where he ministered outside Egypt. A young woman engaged to be married petitioned Abouna to facilitate a wedding rehearsal for her and her bridesmaids, even the flower girls. Abouna was taken aback since the wedding was still six months away. The young woman reasoned those six months was not long, and she had many tasks to accomplish before the nuptials. This experience taught Abouna an invaluable lesson for his spiritual journey. Reflecting on how the young woman deemed it necessary to prepare meticulously for her wedding, he contemplated, "If she, in anticipation of her wedding, feels the need for thorough preparation and rehearsals, how much more should I be prepared for my Bridegroom, who proclaims, *'I am coming quickly'* (Revelation 22:12)"? Thus, he committed to readying himself for the eternal heavenly wedding.

Our Invitation to the Celestial Union

Heaven has long been poised for this celestial union. Our Lord Jesus Christ, through His sacrifice, redeemed His bride—the Church—and offers us His Holy Spirit to refine our souls, preparing us for an eternal union with Him. The twenty-four elders and the heavenly host eagerly await this joyous day when the Bridegroom will be united with His bride.

O Lord, ignite within me an ardent heart that yearns for this joyous occasion. Unveil my eyes and heart to perceive Your coming in Your glorious wedding procession. Lift me with You on a cloud, O Bridegroom of my soul, and present me to Your Father's embrace at the heavenly wedding.

Let us live in constant readiness, inspired by the heavenly promise and the joyous anticipation of being united with our Bridegroom for all eternity.

Chapter 21

The Parable of the Wise, Faithful and Honest Steward

"Watch therefore, for you do not know what hour your Lord is coming, But know this, that if the master of the house had known what hour the thief would come, he would have watched and not allowed his house to be broken into. Therefore you also be ready, for the Son of Man is coming at an hour you do not expect. Who then is a faithful and wise servant, whom his master made ruler over his household, to give them food in due season? Blessed is that servant whom his master, when he comes, will find so doing. Assuredly, I say to you that he will make him ruler over all his goods. But if that evil servant says in his heart, 'My master is delaying his coming, and begins to beat his fellow servants, and to eat and drink with the drunkards, the master of that servant will come on a day when he is not looking for him and at an hour that he is not aware of, and will cut him in two and appoint him his portion with the hypocrites. There shall be weeping and gnashing of teeth" (Matthew 24:42).

In this straightforward parable, Our Lord Jesus poses a significant question: *"Who then is the faithful and wise steward?"* This question was not directed merely to His audience two thousand years ago, but it is for us: Among us, who truly serves as the faithful and prudent steward?

Understanding Stewardship

Let us commence by deciphering the meaning of a steward and what it entails to be stewards. A steward is a caretaker, a manager responsible for another person's affairs, such as their household. But it is imperative to remember that ultimately, the ownership returns to the original possessor. A steward oversees or administers yet is not the owner. A steward must be marked by integrity. So, what do we steward over?

First and foremost, we are stewards of ourselves. Our worth; only Our Lord Jesus Christ can reveal. He alone holds the knowledge about our essence and our value. We likely do not even fully comprehend ourselves, and others close to us may not grasp our distinctive qualities. Yet, Our Lord Jesus Christ knows. Seek Him and, "Lord, what is my value?" A beautiful hymn echoes, "One day, You passed by me. I inquired, 'How much did You pay for me?' You replied, 'I paid much, but My child, it is not too much for you.'"

God proclaims that He expended extensively to redeem us. He humbled Himself, assuming the form of a servant. Do we truly grasp what servitude entails? Likely not, for we have never experienced it. A servant holds no rights and possesses no value. It is akin to dwelling in a house that is not truly yours. I created everything, yet I had no place to lay My head, no food to sustain Me. I depended on others. This is what *"made Himself of no reputation"* (Philippians 2:7) implies.

Do you realize I paid your ransom? On the cross, I bore your penalty. The cross, laden with shame, humiliation, and scorn, was excruciating. Have you lived knowing you would be crucified, executed due to people's denial? Stripped, exposed, a crown of thorns piercing your brow, whipped and pierced—this was your price. Do you comprehend your value to Me?

And this beautiful, irreplaceable person for whom I suffered; I have entrusted to you to return to Me. This is what it means to be stewards of ourselves.

Secondly, we steward those around us—our family, friends, acquaintances and colleagues. They are not accidental; God placed them with us. Our duty is to serve them wholeheartedly. Moreover, we steward our financial resources. Pause and ponder: Are they truly ours, or are they God's? Often, we regard our assets as exclusive possessions, not meant for sharing. Yet, they are entrusted to us. We must be faithful, exercising wisdom in their use.

The Contrast of Stewards: Faithful vs. Wicked

The opposite of the faithful steward is the wicked one, characterized by:

1. Denying the master's return, dulling their conscience, and losing touch with reality through self-indulgence.
2. Sloth—wasting days, months, or even years, forgetting they are accountable for each choice they make.
3. Cruelty—hard-heartedness, injustice, harm to others.

The faithful steward, on the contrary:

1. Remains vigilant, recognizing life's transient nature.
2. Values time, employing it wisely.
3. Embraces kindness, compassion, and love.

Where does faithfulness in the faithful steward originate? In feeling alien to this world, sensing God's presence, knowing accountability for God's gifts. This individual focuses solely on God, values their time and lives prepared for Our Lord Jesus Christ's unexpected return. *"Therefore you also be ready, for the Son of Man is coming at an hour you do not expect."* (Luke 12:40)

My dearest beloved, according to this parable and God's reckoning, there are only two categories:

1. Faithful and wise stewards—humble, unremarkable in worldly terms, yet adorned with the presence of saints and martyrs.
2. Wicked stewards—worldly powerful, indulgent, or negligent.

Whose description matches ours? Are we aligned with the faithful and wise stewards or the wicked ones?

Yours is the glory and honour, now and forever. Amen.

Chapter 22

The Parable of the Ten Virgins

"Then the kingdom of heaven shall be likened to ten virgins who took their lamps and went out to meet the bridegroom. Now five of them were wise, and five were foolish. Those who were foolish took their lamps and took no oil with them, but the wise took oil in their vessels with their lamps. But while the bridegroom was delayed, they all slumbered and slept. *"And at midnight a cry was heard: 'Behold, the bridegroom is coming; go out to meet him!' Then all those virgins arose and trimmed their lamps. And the foolish said to the wise, 'Give us some of your oil, for our lamps are going out.' But the wise answered, saying, 'No, lest there should not be enough for us and you; but go rather to those who sell, and buy for yourselves.' And while they went to buy, the bridegroom came, and those who were ready went in with him to the wedding; and the door was shut.* *"Afterward the other virgins came also, saying, 'Lord, Lord, open to us!' But he answered and said, 'Assuredly, I say to you, I do not know you'* *"Watch therefore, for you know neither the day nor the hour in which the Son of Man is coming."* (Matthew 25:1-13).

A Heavenly call for Watchfulness

This is one of the simplest yet most profound parables, captivating hearts and minds, especially in moments when our spiritual insight is just beginning to awaken. I vividly remember, as a child, feeling deep sorrow when I first heard how the door was shut on the foolish virgins. The weight of their missed opportunity left a lasting impression, teaching the importance of being prepared and vigilant in our walk with God

Unlike other Kingdom parables that start with *"The kingdom of heaven shall be likened to,"* this one begins with *"Then the kingdom of heaven shall be likened to."* The others are in the present tense, but this is in the future tense, directing us towards the future, specifically, the Judgment.

In this parable, the Lord depicts Our Lord Jesus Our Lord Jesus Christ as the bridegroom. St Paul reminds us, *"For I am jealous for you with godly jealousy. For I have betrothed you to one husband, that I may present you as a chaste virgin to Our Lord Jesus Christ"* (2 Corinthians 11:2). Hence, Our Lord Jesus Our Lord Jesus Christ is our bridegroom, and He shall come at midnight to judge the soul. The parable ponders whether His bride will be prepared to meet Him, or unready. The parable implies that those prepared shall go with Him, while those unprepared shall not enter.

The Essential Virtue of Vigilance

All the virgins possessed lamps, yet a vital distinction existed. All dozed, but what varied was their readiness of oil; some held it, others did not. The parable spotlights the Church's readiness. Its central theme is preparedness, and a life lived vigilantly. The Church incorporates this parable, guided by the Holy Spirit, in the Gospel of the First Service of the Midnight Prayer in the Agpeya. It is positioned before initiating the Midnight Praises, urging us to prepare.

The parable's depth encapsulates Our Lord Jesus Christian existence, life lived in Our Lord Jesus Christ It is not an invitation to stand in line to purchase a lamp; genuine Our Lord Jesus Christianity is an ongoing experience. It entails living the Bible, participating in the Church, standing united with fellow believers. Trials, tribulations, grace, victory, joy, defeat, strength, glory are the milestones in our life. They are the oil drops accumulated day by day.

Traditionally, early Church fathers stated that a lamp lasts for two hours before it dims. Thus, every two hours, oil replenishment is required. Monasteries still adhere to this practice; a monk ensures lamps remain fuelled to emit light.

What is the Oil?

Early Church Fathers provided varied interpretations of the oil. Saint John Chrysostom perceived it as almsgiving. Saint Augustine saw it as love. Saint Cyril the Great equated it to the Holy Spirit. Could it be faithfulness or virtuous acts? The oil encapsulates the Our Lord Jesus Christian journey, the life that encompasses spiritual experiences—prayer, spiritual deeds, fasting, scripture study, enduring tribulations for Our Lord Jesus Christ, offering testimonies for Our Lord Jesus Christ the oil embodies our spiritual resources.

In the parable, Our Lord Jesus Christ does not chastise or rebuke the virgins. He highlights that those who had the oil were ready so promptly due to their full oil lamps. At midnight, a call goes, signalling the arrival of the bridegroom. Our Lord Jesus Christ hints at His Second Coming, describing it as happening at midnight. This hour is cherished by hermits and church fathers as it signifies communion with the groom, *"But who can endure the day of His coming? And who can stand when He appears?"* (Malachi 3:2).

Upon the Second Coming, some souls shall rejoice, ready

to meet Him, while others shall not be prepared. In the parable, all virgins arose and trimmed their lamps. A time of fear and tension transpires for the foolish virgins who implore the wise, "Give us some of your oil, for our lamps are going out." Here lies a question: Can one share their oil with another? As previously mentioned, oil symbolizes love, hope, faith, patience, perseverance, living with our Lord Jesus Christ the theological response is no; there's just enough oil for oneself, impossible to share. A virtue cannot be bought; it is acquired through effort, prayer, tribulations, struggles, fasting, vigilance, tolerance, enduring persecution. All these constitute the oil, and it is un-sharable.

Our faith teaches us that one cannot redeem another. Salvation is individual, and oil accumulates drop by drop daily. Some days pass without collecting drops, other days we deplete our reservoir, burning it swiftly when frustration, anger, judgment, dishonesty emerge. This is why we must collect oil daily.

Where do we gather oil? Plenty surrounds us—the poor, sick, lonely, the prisoned, the sad and troubled people, our personal prayer corner. Opening our Bible daily adds oil drops. Living a Christian life—embracing commandments, forgiving, loving, humility—multiplies the oil. It is abundant around us, though some might not see it.

Others, however, remain vigilant, awake, spending nights with their bridegroom, never growing weary of turning their gaze toward heaven, echoing, *"I will lift up my eyes to the hills, from whence comes my help"* (Psalm 121:1). Their hearts and desires remain undiminished by their position at their groom's feet.

In the first century Christianity, it was customary, at the end of the liturgy, for all believers to proclaim in unison, "Maranatha [The Lord is coming]! O Come Lord Our Lord Jesus Our Lord Jesus Christ quickly, and the world will end." This practice deeply rooted the early Church in Our Lord Jesus Christ the Bridegroom. Contrast this with today, where hearts and minds often feel cold. Some resist even a 15-minute encounter with the Bible or prayer. Among us are both foolish and wise individuals—some zealously engaged in a rich spiritual journey, filling their lamps with oil, while others neglect their spiritual well-being, oblivious to the swiftness of passing time.

The Parable's Heartbreaking Part

The parable's critical point concerning the foolish virgins is that the door is closed on them. Their time has completed. Just as Matthew 24:41 describes, *"Two women will be grinding at the mill: one will be taken and the other left."* Long ago, I felt this was unfair and lacked mercy. But now we understand the reason, and it is made clear by their lives. One soul lived immersed in the Bible, continually at the feet of Our Lord Jesus the Teacher, like Mary, *"Mary has chosen that good part, which will not be taken away from her"* (Luke 10:42). They prayed, lit candles, detached from worldly desires, shed tears, prostrated, prayed for others, communed with Our Lord Jesus, fasted, ardently longed for Our Lord Jesus Christ, resembling the wise virgins. In contrast, another soul wandered aimlessly in the world, squandering life, refusing to gather oil, indulging in desires, and living idly, unfulfilled, and unaware.

The highlight for all of us in this harsh part of the parable lies in the Bridegroom's unannounced arrival, devoid of a given time, introduction, or preparation. In my youth, I believed the Lord should provide warnings or signs. Yet as I matured, God's grace unveiled the truth—every moment passing in our life is a warning; each sermon we hear and opportunity to serve is a warning.

This parable's message is a warning: be wary of the shutting of the door; for life terminates, opportunities conclude, and the chance to awaken and to replenish oil ends.

The foolish virgins pleaded, *"Master, Master, open to*

us." The opportunity had ended. The parable wisely employs the term "Master." Formerly, we called Him "Our Father", but now, He's the Master and the Just Judge. In the Agpeya, we constantly acknowledge, "Behold, I am about to stand before the Just Judge." Our lives resonate with, "Behold, the bridegroom comes at midnight, blessed is the servant whom He finds awake." The door is knocked upon, but alas, the chance is missed.

The parable's most heartbreaking part is, *"Assuredly, I say to you, I do not know you."* Oh Lord, after so many years on earth, is that true? Yes, it is for those who did not know the truth, who did not count days, for whom time has slipped away. Thus, He commands us to *"Watch."* This is the crucial advice we must frame in gold and place before our eyes. This prescription is what God has administered to us. The Church echoes it continually: WATCH. Our confession fathers reiterate: WATCH. Be vigilant, accumulate oil in your lamps, repent, and confess, battle. Be confident that one step taken will grant grace for ten more. Blessed is the soul that remains watchful, ready, wise, and vigilant. We must impart this vigilance to our children.

The Path to Heaven: Wisdom's Essential Role

A remarkable story of our Church concerns Sophia (meaning wisdom) who raised three daughters named Agapy (love), Pestis (faith), and Helpis (hope). Wisdom guided her to instil

vigilance in them. Despite their tender ages—9, 10, and 12—she readied them for martyrdom. Sophia cultivated faith within them, granting them strength to endure and stand firm when torture befell them.

Let us conclude with the poignant words the Church presents in the First Service of the Midnight Prayer in the Agpeya, urging our souls: *"Remember my soul that awesome day, awake and light your lamp with the oil of joy. You do not know when the voice will call: 'Behold, here comes the bridegroom.' Watch, my soul, lest you fall asleep and remain outside knocking like the five foolish virgins. Watch with prayers to meet the Lord, Our Lord Jesus Christ, with rich oil. He will bestow upon you the joys of His divine glory."*

May God grant you and me a life of wakefulness, readiness, and vigilance, so we may stand with the wise virgins, our lamps filled with oil gathered throughout our lives.

Yours is the glory and honour, now and forever. Amen.

Chapter 23

The Parable of the Talents

"For the kingdom of heaven is like a man traveling to a far country, who called his own servants and delivered his goods to them. And to one he gave five talents, to another two, and to another one, to each according to his own ability; and immediately he went on a journey. Then he who had received the five talents went and traded with them, and made another five talents. And likewise he who had received two gained two more also. But he who had received one went and dug in the ground, and hid his lord's money. After a long time the lord of those servants came and settled accounts with them. So he who had received five talents came and brought five other talents, saying, 'Lord, you delivered to me five talents; look, I have gained five more talents besides them.' His lord said to him, 'Well done, good and faithful servant; you were faithful over a few things, I will make you ruler over many things. Enter into the joy of your lord.' He also who had received two talents came and said, 'Lord, you delivered to me two talents; look, I have gained two more talents besides them.' His lord said to him, 'Well done, good and faithful servant; you have been faithful over a few things, I will make you ruler over many things. Enter into the joy of your lord.' "Then he who had received the one talent came and said, 'Lord, I knew you to be a hard man, reaping where you have not sown, and gathering where you have not scattered seed. And I was afraid, and went and hid your talent in the ground. Look, there you have what is yours.'

"But his lord answered and said to him, 'You wicked and lazy servant, you knew that I reap where I have not sown, and gather where I have not scattered seed. So you ought to have deposited my money with the bankers, and at my coming I would have received back my own with interest. So take the talent from him, and give it to him who has ten talents. 'For to everyone who has, more will be given, and he will have abundance; but from him who does not have, even what he has will be taken away. And cast the unprofitable servant into the outer darkness. There will be weeping and gnashing of teeth.' (Matthew 25:14-30).

Understanding the Parable

This final parable from the Gospel according Saint Matthew is a profound lesson about the Kingdom of Heaven. It is the core of Our Lord Jesus' teachings, offering insight into our eternal salvation. Without understanding this parable, we might resemble the servant who buried his talent in the ground instead of using it.

This parable presents two options: standing with the faithful and honest servant, or with the wicked and lazy servant. The decision is yours.

This parable, read during Holy Week and is the gospel read in our church during the funeral service of priests, starts with two important notes:
1. Goods delivered to them - reminding us that our possessions belong to God, just as the master delivered to his servants.

2. According to their ability - God grants talents according to our abilities, recognizing what we can and cannot do. It is not the quantity, but how much we trade and gain.

In the past, a talent was equal to 25 kilograms of gold or 6000 Dirham. One Dirham equalled a day's work. So, one talent was about 30 years of work. This illustrates God's trust in us. The grace of the Holy Spirit within us is the greatest gift.

Lessons from the Parable

As Saint Paul the Apostle wrote in his Romans epistle, God gifts various talents: wisdom, healing, faith, power, discernment, and each talent serves the body of Our Lord Jesus Christ, and thus should never be abused for selfish gain or to esteem oneself in the eyes of others. God's gifts are for the construction and strengthening of the Church. For instance, Saint Paul had knowledge and a great mind, while Saint Peter had enthusiasm and zeal. Elijah possessed zeal, Moses displayed meekness, and Jeremiah embodied sensitivity. Job embodied patience, and John the Baptist exhibited self-denial. Abraham had faith, Joseph the Righteous had purity. The gifts differ but share common themes:

- Appreciating and understanding the talent.
- Surrendering it to God.
- Remaining faithful and honest
- This leads to gain.

Therefore, do not compare yourself to others. Use what God has given you. It is essential to understand and return it to God's hands with honesty, and you will gain.

Stewardship and Faithfulness

In the Coptic Orthodox tradition, the Parable of the Talents is understood as a teaching on stewardship, accountability, and the proper use of God-given gifts and abilities. Here is a summary of how the Coptic Orthodox Church interprets this parable:

1. **Stewardship of God's Gifts:** The talents in the parable represent not only material possessions but also spiritual gifts, abilities, and opportunities that God entrusts to His people. Each servant receives talents according to his ability, highlighting the uniqueness of God's gifts to individuals.

2. **Responsibility and Accountability:** The parable emphasizes the responsibility of believers to use their talents wisely and productively. God expects His servants to actively engage in His work, invest their gifts for His kingdom, and contribute to the growth of His purposes on earth.

3. **Faithfulness and Diligence:** The servants who invest their talents and produce a return demonstrate faithfulness, diligence, and initiative in serving their master. Their actions reflect a deep trust in God's provision and a desire to honour him with their efforts.

4. **Consequences of Inaction:** The servant who buries his talent out of fear represents a failure to recognize the value of his master's investment and a lack of faith in God's ability to bless his efforts. His inaction leads to condemnation, highlighting the seriousness of neglecting God-given opportunities and gifts.

5. **Reward and Punishment:** The master's response to each servant's actions underscores the principle of divine judgment and accountability. Those who are faithful and productive are rewarded with greater responsibilities and blessings, while those who are

negligent face consequences for their actions.

6. **Encouragement to Faithfulness:** The parable serves as an exhortation for believers to use their talents wisely, invest in God's kingdom, and live with a sense of accountability before God. It reminds them that God has entrusted them with gifts for His purposes and expects them to be faithful stewards of His blessings.

The parable first deals with the servant who received 5 talents. Unlike the 11th-hour parable, this servant is expected to achieve much. God asks more from those given more *"For everyone to whom much is given, from him much will be required; and to whom much has been committed, of him they will ask the more" (Luke 12:48)*. If God grants you much, be wary, for He demands more. Think of the great prophets and saints of our Church that God blessed and revealed Himself to, and then think of how much they suffered for His name.

The key to the Kingdom? Faithfulness. As Mother Teresa beautifully said, 'God has not called me to be successful. He called me to be faithful.' Faithfulness is the invaluable key that opens the doors of God's Kingdom, transforming even the smallest talent into a multitude. A faithful servant remains committed in all things, whether great or small—in spirit, relationships, service, prayer, confession, Bible study, work, tithes, thoughts, and heart. Faithfulness means fully embracing and using all the talents God has given us. It is an undivided life; you cannot be faithful in one area while neglecting another. True faithfulness permeates every aspect of our lives. By observing and learning from faithful individuals around us, we grow; being faithful in one area naturally leads us to faithfulness in another. This is how we mature and deepen in the life of faithfulness

Examine the talents God bestowed upon you. Consider if you have traded with them, and if you are aware of the kingdom. Your reward in heaven depends on your trading, struggling, and gaining. Judgment is not on those who tried and failed; it is on those who did not try and hid their talents.

The servant who hid his talent is called "wicked." This represents the unrepentant sinner. Hiding the talent obstructs grace's work in life due to:

1. Ignorance or neglect of the talent's value.
2. Forgetting life's mission and purpose, consumed by worldly affairs.
3. Loss of love; an empty heart signifies distance from God. The wicked servant accused his master saying, *"I knew you to be a hard man,"* but this was the hardness of his own heart.

The second part of the parable deals with judgment. We stand before God, who is both, merciful and just we must obey God's words and live according to His teachings.

A true story illustrates that even a small talent is precious to God, as seen in the widow and her two mites. Years ago, before I have graced by God to unworthy receive the gift of priesthood, I knew a Greek lady named Maria, a school janitor, who would give a coin to children and say, "Our Lord Jesus loves you." Years later, she came to my workplace clearly very emotional with tears in her eyes. This was during Holy Week, and the Greek tradition encourages an extremely strict fast for the week. She had just arrived home from her Pascha service, ready to eat a meagre meal of a small piece of bread, when a young man had knocked on her door, asking her for any food. She invited him in and told her she was happy to share her bread with him. As she returned from preparing a drink for him, he saw him praying by the table with the bread raised in the air, where she could clearly see the wounds on his hands. He then vanished, and she was overcome with emotion and felt compelled to share this holy encounter; and each time she shared the story afterwards, she would again be overwhelmed with tears. Her small acts of love she had shown those children were entrusted directly back into God's hands.

Overall, the Parable of the Talents emphasizes the importance of faithful stewardship, active engagement in

God's work, and the accountability that believers have before God for the use of their gifts and abilities. It encourages believers to recognize the value of God's investments in their lives and to respond with diligence, faithfulness, and trust in His provision.

May God make us good and faithful servants, hearing His voice as we take our last breath, saying, *"Well done, good and faithful servant; you have been faithful over a few things, I will make you ruler over many things. Enter into the joy of your Lord"* (Matthew 25:23).

Yours is the glory and honour, now and forever. Amen.

Chapter 24

The Parable of the Good Samaritan

"And behold, a certain lawyer stood up and tested Him, saying, "Teacher, what shall I do to inherit eternal life?"

He said to him, "What is written in the law? What is your reading of it?"

So he answered and said, "You shall love the **Lord** your God with all your heart, with all your soul, with all your strength, and with all your mind,' and 'your neighbour as yourself.'"

And He said to him, "You have answered rightly; do this and you will live."

But he, wanting to justify himself, said to Our Lord Jesus, "And who is my neighbour?"

Then Our Lord Jesus answered and said: "A certain man went down from Jerusalem to Jericho, and fell among thieves, who stripped him of his clothing, wounded him, and departed, leaving him half dead. Now by chance a certain priest came down that road. And when he saw him, he passed by on the other side. Likewise a Levite, when he arrived at the place, came and looked, and passed by on the *other side. But a certain Samaritan, as he journeyed, came where he was. And when he saw him, he had compassion. So he went to him and bandaged his wounds, pouring on oil and wine; and he set him on his own animal, brought him to an inn, and took care of him. On the next day, when he departed, he took out two denarii, gave them to the innkeeper, and said to him, 'Take care of him; and whatever more you spend, when I come again, I will repay you.' So which of these three do you think was neighbour to him who fell among the thieves?"*

And he said, "He who showed mercy on him." Then Our Lord Jesus said to him, "Go and do likewise." (Luke 10:25-37).

Understanding the Parable: The Journey of Compassion

This parable stands as the apex of Saint Luke's Gospel, and in my very humble opinion, it is the most exquisite narrative shared by Our Lord Jesus Christ. The Early Church Fathers often engaged in discussions about it. Let us explore its analysis in greater detail.

A Pharisee asked Our Lord Jesus about entering the Kingdom of Heaven. Remember, our life's goal is eternity. Our Lord Jesus responded by acknowledging the Pharisee's knowledge of the commandments due to his upbringing. However, Our Lord Jesus Christ wanted to stress that memorizing is not enough; ascending from intellectual knowledge to practical living is essential. This transformation is crucial for us as well – to translate the commandments from the mind to the heart. The Pharisee memorized but did not live them. His problem lay here.

When the Pharisee inquired about his neighbour, we too should question ourselves – "Who is my neighbour?" Your heart's size determines your answer. If your heart is small, your neighbour includes immediate family; a slightly larger

The Parable of the Good Samaritan

heart embraces friends; an even bigger heart encompasses neighbours and colleagues. The largest heart loves even enemies. The Word of God illuminates the soul: *"Your word is a lamp unto my feet"* (Psalm 119:105).

Our Lord Jesus tells of a man who fell victim to thieves on the road from Jerusalem to Jericho. They robbed, wounded, and left him for dead. A priest and a Levite saw him and walked past A Samaritan, regardless of his faith or background, stopped. Our Lord Jesus Christ illustrates that our neighbour encompasses all humanity. The heart, like a sponge, expands with love – if we fill it with love, God grants us more love.

This Samaritan saw the wounded man, showing compassion. "Compassion" requires divine assistance and always comes ultimately from Our Lord Jesus' own immense compassion for others. It is not just about feeling; it necessitates action – treating wounds and aiding the person. Compassion involves deeds, not just words or tears.

Throughout my life growing in the Coptic Orthodox tradition, I have always learned and witnessed the Parable of the Good Samaritan is interpreted as a lesson on compassion, love for neighbour, and the true meaning of righteousness irrespective of colour, race, sex, background it is infinite dimension for the love of God as saint Paul expressed in his astonishing words guided by The Holy Spirit *"that He would grant you, according to the riches of His glory, to be strengthened with might through His Spirit in the inner man, that Christ may dwell in your hearts through faith; that you, being rooted and grounded in love, may be able to comprehend with all the saints what is the width and length and depth and height— to know the love of Christ which passes knowledge; that you may be filled with all the fullness of God." Ephesians 3:18-21*

Here is a summary of how the Coptic Orthodox Church views this parable:

1. **Compassionate Action:** The parable teaches the importance of compassionate action towards those

in need, regardless of their social status, ethnicity, or background. The Samaritan, traditionally viewed as an outsider or enemy by the Jewish audience, demonstrates genuine care and mercy towards the wounded man, exemplifying the Christian call to love one's neighbour as oneself.

2. **Neighbourly Love:** The parable challenges the narrow definition of "neighbour" and expands it to include anyone in need of help, regardless of religious, cultural, or societal differences. It emphasizes that true neighbourly love transcends boundaries and requires selfless sacrifice and kindness towards all individuals, even those who may be considered enemies or outsiders.

3. **Model of Christ-like Love:** The Samaritan's actions mirror the selfless love and compassion of Christ, who came to earth to seek and save the lost. His willingness to sacrifice his time, resources, and comfort for the sake of a stranger exemplifies the sacrificial love that Christians are called to emulate in their lives.

4. **Call to Active Engagement:** The parable challenges believers to actively engage in acts of mercy, compassion, and social justice in their communities. It emphasizes the importance of being attentive to the needs of others, responding with empathy and generosity, and seeking to alleviate suffering and injustice wherever it is found.

5. **Eternal Life Through Love:** Jesus concludes the parable by instructing the lawyer to "go and do likewise," highlighting the connection between loving actions and inheriting eternal life. The parable teaches that genuine love and compassion towards others are essential components of true righteousness and are central to experiencing the fullness of life in God's kingdom.

The Model of Christ-like Love

Many need such compassionate deeds in their lives – those burdened with agony, in pain, and upset. Listening without judgment – carrying others' burdens with them – is an act of love. Being compassionate implies setting ego aside, as ego is our greatest enemy. When consumed with self, we lack the ability to see others' pain. This parable teaches boundary-free love, encouraging us to love expansively and give, aiming for the Kingdom and eternal life. Store as much love in your lamp as possible.

This parable symbolizes Our Lord Jesus' descent with boundless love. He is the Good Samaritan who collected wounded souls affected by sin, carrying them to the Church and binding their wounds.

Living Out the Parable: The Call to Compassionate Action

Christian life is not lived haphazardly, aimlessly, or randomly but is guided by a standard or guideline, primarily found in the Holy Bible. While our Lord Jesus did not provide a new set of rules like the Ten Commandments, He emphasized the commandment of love and often used parables to convey moral messages. The parables teach that Christianity is a calling and a duty, requiring trust in God's word, honest labour, and reflection of God's love through actions. The duty of the Christian is to work diligently, recognizing that all talents come from God, and to reflect God's love to others, even in difficult circumstances. Ultimately, the Christian is called to serve with love, guided by the teachings of Christ and the principles revealed through His parables.

A story told to me by Fr Bishoy Botros illustrates this. A devout woman with a spacious house invited neighbours for Sunday Bible studies. One day, she found a man near her car who seemed to be trying to break in. Instead of reacting harshly, she offered food and money, inviting him into her home. He noticed the cross hanging from her guest room and asked about it, and she spoke about to him about Christ and invited him to their Bible study. He joined the Bible study, and quickly became a regular who would arrive early and assist with preparing it each Sunday. Through her act of love, he was transformed from a thief into a devoted participant. That same lady was diagnosed with a terminal case of cancer, and despite her pain, sufferings, and the heavy medication she was receiving, she would travel around the hospital wards to share the great message of hope in the Gospel.

Our Lord is present in every moment and place, witnessing our every step. When we walk faithfully in His light and live with a heart full of love, we begin to reflect His divine nature—transforming our hearts, minds, and spirits to mirror His grace and goodness

May God grant us compassionate hearts, filling them with His love and Holy Spirit.

Yours is the glory and honour, now and forever. Amen.

Chapter 25

The Parable of the Friend at Midnight

"Now it came to pass, as He was praying in a certain place, when He ceased, that one of His disciples said to Him, "Lord, teach us to pray, as John also taught his disciples."

So He said to them, "When you pray, say: Our Father in heaven, Hallowed be Your name. Your kingdom come. Your will be done On earth as it is in heaven. Give us day by day our daily bread. And forgive us our sins, For we also forgive everyone who is indebted to us. And do not lead us into temptation, But deliver us from the evil one." And He said to them, "Which of you shall have a friend, and go to him at midnight and say to him, 'Friend, lend me three loaves; for a friend of mine has come to me on his journey, and I have nothing to set before him'; and he will answer from within and say, 'Do not trouble me; the door is now shut, and my children are with me in bed; I cannot rise and give to you'? I say to you, though he will not rise and give to him because he is his friend, yet because of his persistence he will rise and give him as many as he needs.

"So I say to you, ask, and it will be given to you; seek, and you will find; knock, and it will be opened to you. For everyone *who asks receives, and he who seeks finds, and to him who knocks it will be opened. If a son asks for bread from any father among you, will he give him a stone? Or if he asks for a fish, will he give him a serpent instead of a fish? Or if he asks for an egg, will he offer him a scorpion? If you then, being evil, know how to give good gifts to your children, how much more will your heavenly Father give the Holy Spirit to those who ask Him!" (Luke 11:1-13).*

Our Lord Jesus Christ took great care in imparting this parable to His disciples and all believers, likening it to the struggle of prayer with God. This is a significant aspect of our spiritual life, exemplified by the desert fathers who centred their lives on prayer.

Prayer goes beyond simple requests; our forefathers referred to it as the "life of prayer" or a prayer curriculum that grows day by day, gained through standing before God and wrestling with Him in our prayer room. The term "pour out" is crucial in prayer. It signifies revealing what is within us, encountering God, and allowing His light to illuminate our hearts. The devil targets our prayer life, allowing us to listen to sermons, read spiritual books, or watch videos, but he cannot tolerate our commitment to prayer. He aims to disrupt it, fighting against our progress.

Our Lord Jesus introduces three kinds of friends in this parable:

The first friend who was traveling during the day but faced nightfall before he was ready. He remembered an old friend's house, and, despite his shame at having to impose, boldly went to this friend's house to ask him for a favour. This passing from day to sudden night symbolises our spiritual journey from light to darkness due to negligence and Satan's snares. We must remember those spiritual guides – priests, servants and friends –, who bring us back to Our Lord Jesus Christ's bosom, similar to the friend's home, at midnight.

The second friend – the owner of the house – is the one who welcomed the traveller in the middle of the night without questioning his lateness. He did not think of the impropriety of his friend's behaviour or scold his ridiculous request but took him in and saw only to his needs. This is the calling of all of us who are servants, and even beyond. This friend represents those who compassionately accept us in our time of need, even at inconvenient times, without judgment. And these friends, when we have them, are irreplaceable treasures.

The third friend initially declined the request due to the late hour, but eventually opened the door due to the persistence of his knocking. This is the essence of this parable: the value of persistence in prayer. The third friend represents the Lord, who allows us to wear Him down with determination, especially the repentance of sinners and those in need, to whom He says, *"Come to Me, all you who labor and are heavy laden, and I will give you rest"* (Matthew 11:28).

The Key word: Persistence

Persistence in prayer means more than simple repetition of words; it involves standing before God with a deep sense of need. It is knowing that only God can hear you, and only He can help you, and so you will not leave until He responds. Think of Jacob who so audaciously said, *"I will not let You go until You bless me!"* (Genesis 32:26). It is tempting to become exasperated with God for sometimes asking us to persist before He answers our prayers – if He already knows our needs and loves us, why would He require this tedious, slow process? It is not difficult to imagine what some reasons might be – perhaps He is allowing us to see the limit of our faith, or to teach us humility in humbling ourselves before Him if we have started to view Him as a genie who will freely grant our wishes. Perhaps He is simply trying to teach us the determination needed to withstand temptation: *"Blessed be the Lord my Rock, Who trains my hands for war and my fingers for battle"* (Psalm 144:1). As we wrestle with Him, over time, our prayer room experience teaches us how to speak to Him as a friend, fostering intimacy, love, trust, and shameless vulnerability.

his parable culminates with the transition from friend to son. In comparing God's dealings with us to a child requesting from his father, Our Lord Jesus Christ reminds us that our relationship with God is more than just a friend whom we have to pester to get him to care about our needs, but that He is a loving Father who delights in helping us. The parable opens three windows: asking, seeking, and knocking, which allow us to approach God persistently and with need, seeking the Holy Spirit. These windows lead us to ask for the Holy Spirit for ourselves, loved ones, and our homes.

May we all be filled with the Holy Spirit, individually, in our families, and in our homes.

Yours is the glory and honour, now and forever. Amen.

Chapter 26

The Parable of the Foolish Rich Man

"Then one from the crowd said to Him, "Teacher, tell my brother to divide the inheritance with me." But He said to him, "Man, who made Me a judge or an arbitrator over you?" And He said to them, "Take heed and beware of covetousness, for one's life does not consist in the abundance of the things he possesses." Then He spoke a parable to them, saying: "The ground of a certain rich man yielded plentifully. And he thought within himself, saying, 'What shall I do, since I have no room to store my crops?' So he said, 'I will do this: I will pull down my barns and build greater, and there I will store all my crops and my goods. And I will say to my soul, "Soul, you have many goods laid up for many years; take your ease; eat, drink, and be merry." But God said to him, 'Fool! This night your soul will be required of you; then whose will those things be which you have provided?' "So is he who lays up treasure for himself, and is not rich toward God." (Luke 12:13).

Our Lord Our Lord Jesus, in many of His teachings, cautions against greed, the love of money, and self-indulgence. The pursuit of worldly desires and material possessions is not aligned with God's will, as *"all that is in the world—the lust of the flesh, the lust of the eyes, and the pride of life—is not of the Father but is of the world"* (1 John 2:16).

At the beginning of creation, God had a profound purpose for Adam, which was marred by his greed. Adam's desire to create a separate identity apart from God led to a departure from God's original plan. Similarly, humanity often seeks independence from God, even though our value, eternity, security, and protection are found in Our Lord Jesus Christ alone. St Paul repeatedly emphasizes being "in Our Lord Jesus Christ" about 150 times in his epistles.

The parable highlights a man who, consumed by greed, focused on his possessions and self-indulgence. Like him, we often prioritize material wealth over spiritual riches, ignoring the fleeting nature of possessions. This short-sightedness drives us to accumulate more and more, disregarding the fact that we cannot take our possessions with us. Our Lord Jesus Christ, using the term "fool," rebukes this man for his lack of spiritual insight.

The man's words reveal the depth of his foolishness:

1. In saying, *"I have no room to store my crops,"* He spoke of his possessions without acknowledging God's role in providing them.

2. *"I will say to my soul, "Soul, you have many goods laid up for many years; take your ease; eat, drink, and be merry"."* He presumed a long life ahead, indulging in ease and temporary pleasures. You have many years ahead of you? Who decided that? Is your life in your own hands, or the hands of your riches? Is long life a reward for earthly success? Or, dear fool, do these gifts come from above, and are they all in God's hands? Every breath we take is a gift from God. We constantly pray, "Give us this day or daily bread," because we know that regardless of who grew the wheat, baked the loaf, or sold the bread, every meal is provided by God, and the next one is never guaranteed. This is not

even considering his complete overlooking of his poor neighbour and disregard for any charitable works. God blesses you, and you feed your storehouses rather than the hungry?

3. *"I will pull down my barns and build greater."* His solution to excess was not to donate it or to find a way to spend it wisely. A bulging storehouse was not an indicator that he had enough, but that he did not have enough space. Imagine eating a meal that is much more than you can eat and deciding that the solution was to expand your stomach. This man sees only himself and his own needs, and any energy or resources spent on someone else is only ever wasted.

I will leave you to decide if he has earned the label of 'fool'. The thing I appreciate most in this parable is Our Lord Jesus' words. They are harsh, but He does not immediately take the man's life. Instead, Our Lord Jesus Christ grants a chance for repentance, demonstrating God's desire for sinners to turn back to Him. The warning highlights God's patience and mercy, as He waits for us to come to our senses and change our ways, as He is the God *"Who desires all men to be saved and to come to the knowledge of the truth"* (1 Timothy 2:4).

The parable's message resonates with us, urging us to prioritise God over materialism. We are reminded that life is not merely about indulging in comforts, but about aligning with God's purpose and being rich in a spiritual sense. The parable's hope lies in God's patience and second chances, showing that even when we stray, God waits for us to return.

Dear brethren, we encounter people intentionally placed by God in our lives for mutual blessings. Let us shift our focus from self-indulgence to aiding those in need, understanding that true security lies in Our Lord Jesus Christ, not our possessions. As we strive to be rich in God, let us recognize that all our belongings are ultimately His, meant to glorify Him.

Yours is the glory and honour, now and forever. Amen.

Chapter 27

The Parable of the Unjust Steward

"He also said to His disciples: "There was a certain rich man who had a steward, and an accusation was brought to him that this man was wasting his goods. So he called him and said to him, 'What is this I hear about you? Give an account of your stewardship, for you can no longer be steward.'

"Then the steward said within himself, 'What shall I do? For my master is taking the stewardship away from me. I cannot dig; I am ashamed to beg. I have resolved what to do, that when I am put out of the stewardship, they may receive me into their houses.'

"So he called every one of his master's debtors to him, and said to the first, 'How much do you owe my master?' And he said, 'A hundred measures of oil.' So he said to him, 'Take your bill, and sit down quickly and write fifty.' Then he said to another, 'And how much do you owe?' So he said, 'A hundred measures of wheat.' And he said to him, 'Take your bill, and write eighty.' So the master commended the unjust steward because he had dealt shrewdly. For the sons of this world are more shrewd in their generation than the sons of light.

The Parable of the Unjust Steward

"And I say to you, make friends for yourselves by unrighteous mammon, that when you fail, they may receive you into an everlasting home. He who is faithful in what is least is faithful also in much; and he who is unjust in what is least is unjust also in much. therefore, if you have not been faithful in the unrighteous mammon, who will commit to your trust the true riches? And if you have not been faithful in what is another man's, who will give you what is your own?

"No servant can serve two masters; for either he will hate the one and love the other, or else he will be loyal to the one and despise the other. You cannot serve God and mammon." (Luke 16:1-13).

The interpretations of this parable by the Early Church Fathers and theologians have varied, with different focuses on its message. Origen suggested understanding the overarching idea rather than delving into specifics. Both Saint John Chrysostom and Saint Augustine, renowned for their concern for the poor, emphasized befriending unrighteous mammon through service to the needy. Similarly, Saint Cyril the Great emphasized that money should be used to serve the poor.

The term "unrighteous mammon" similarly has different interpretations. Some view it as unused money meant for serving others. Others relate it to God's money, referring to tithing. Some believe that all money in the world, as it stays within the worldly cycle, can be considered unrighteous mammon.

The matters of this world – the 'mammon' – involve the worldly systems and powers that govern financial markets, politics, and economic transactions. And consider how Our Lord Jesus Christ frequently identifies the ruler of this world as Satan, it follows that these things also might be considered, "unrighteous mammon." The steward is identified as you and me, and the friends represent the poor and oppressed.

The parable's core message is about the transition to eternity. Our Lord Jesus Christ prompts listeners to shift their focus from the temporal to the eternal, encouraging them to "sell" worldly attachments to gain heavenly treasures. The steward's shrewdness becomes a metaphor for trading worldly concerns for eternal rewards.

This teaching emphasizes wisdom and faithfulness, echoing previous parables. The call to be faithful stewards resonates, reflecting the notion of being trustworthy with the resources, talents, and time allotted during our earthly journey. The earthly principles of investment and wise decision-making are highlighted, as they influence our heavenly outcomes. The shrewd steward saw his opportunity, and he took it.

The parable underscores that in the Kingdom, the way things are valued and assessed may differ from earthly standards. It urges adherence to the singular path leading to heaven, while the ultimate destination remains a mystery. The three crucial points to grasp are that we are stewards of God's resources that faithful living is vital for eternal reward, and that wise decision-making is key to heavenly accounting.

May we all become wise and faithful stewards of the resources entrusted to us, that we may hear the beautiful words of Our Lord Jesus Christ that we all yearn for: *"Well done good and faithful servant."*

Yours is the glory and honour, both now and forever. Amen

Chapter 28

The Parable of the Fig Tree - Part 2

"There were present at that season some who told Him about the Galileans whose blood Pilate had mingled with their sacrifices. And Our Lord Jesus answered and said to them, "Do you suppose that these Galileans were worse sinners than all other Galileans, because they suffered such things? I tell you, no; but unless you repent you will all likewise perish. Or those eighteen on whom the tower in Siloam fell and killed them, do you think that they were worse sinners than all other men who dwelt in Jerusalem? I tell you, no; but unless you repent you will all likewise perish."

He also spoke this parable: "A certain man had a fig tree planted in his vineyard, and he came seeking fruit on it and found none. Then he said to the keeper of his vineyard, 'Look, for three years I have come seeking fruit on this fig tree and find none. Cut it down; why does it use up the ground?' But he answered and said to him, 'Sir, let it alone this year also, until I dig around it and fertilize it. And if it bears fruit, well. But if not, after that you can cut it down.'" (Luke 13:1-9).

This parable begins with a master inspecting a fig tree in his vineyard. Upon finding no fruit on the tree, he instructs the vineyard keeper to cut it down. However, the keeper pleads for one more year to nurture it. This parable holds a personalized message for each of us, like a private letter with a "private and confidential" stamp. It is as if God sends daily messages, beckoning us to return to Him, carry our crosses, and follow Him.

In the context of this parable, God has been seeking fruit from our lives for years, symbolized by the fig tree. Although we may outwardly appear vibrant with leaves, representing a semblance of spirituality, the absence of fruit suggests a lack of genuine spiritual growth. This raises the question: What constitutes the "fruit" in our lives? To answer this, honest introspection is required. Honesty means confronting our deficiencies head-on, much like a CT scan revealing every detail. For example, if we struggle to love someone, we should admit it instead of masking it as merely avoiding them. If forgiveness is difficult, we should acknowledge the struggle rather than pretending it does not exist we must admit these difficulties if we have any chance of overcoming them.

The parable pivots to the core theme: the love God seeks from us. Often, we love those who reciprocate or enhance our status or self-esteem. However, as we all know, Our Lord Jesus Christ says to *"Love your enemies, bless those who curse you, do good to those who hate you"* (Matthew 5:44). The Devil tempts us to make excuses for withholding love, but when we place these excuses on one side of the scale and the command to love on the other, the choice should lean toward Our Lord Jesus Christ's command. Do not misunderstand; there are many people who can make loving them exceedingly difficult. Those who talk about us behind our backs, actively work against our goals, and those who betray us. But it is also clear that it is these who make Our Lord Jesus Christ's command so profound. These are our "enemies," and we must love them.

Similarly, forgiveness is vital for spiritual growth. While there might be "logical" reasons to withhold forgiveness, doing so can lead to misery and hinder our growth. Grudges fester like a disease that produces a cruel heart. And cruelty, whether intentional or through neglect, never yields happiness. Instead, it causes pain and becomes a stumbling block to both our spiritual progress and the well-being of others. To cut off a friend in retaliation for some offence is one of the harshest punishments we can inflict. It tells them that they are not even worth listening to. If it has ever happened to you, you will know how painful it is, and how it can bring a great sadness upon our souls; affecting our sleep and demoralising us in our daily lives. So why then should I inflict this upon my brother or sister? Only Satan rejoices in divisions like this.

God's voice and Satan's voice may clash within us. By listening to God's voice and choosing love and forgiveness, we bring joy to heaven, glorify God, and foster reconciliation. Neglecting these virtues, on the other hand, grieves heaven and obstructs our own spiritual growth as well as that of others.

The parable underscores that time is limited, urging us to be honest about our lives. If we have lost the fear of God, we must reclaim it. We must measure our relationship with God, our choices, actions, services, repentance, and relationships with others. In our quiet moments with God, we can open our hearts to Him, make decisions that align with His will, and strive to implement them.

This may be a harsh message today, and it may sting, but I fear that we are losing the fear of God in our lives. We sin without a second thought, and God's voice has become just an annoying noise in the back of our minds. But God said, *"My sheep know My voice"* (John 10:27). If indeed we are His sheep, we must hear His voice and obey Him. As St Paul says, *"And do this, knowing the time, that now it is high time to awake out of sleep; for now our salvation is nearer than when we first believed. The night is far spent, the day is at hand. Therefore let us cast off the works of darkness, and let us put on the armour of light"* (Romans 13:11).

Ultimately, the parable emphasizes that the Kingdom of Heaven is invaluable. To enter it, we must cultivate the image of Our Lord Jesus Christ within us, manifested through love and service to others. Just as Our Lord Jesus Christ washed the feet of His disciples, we should humble ourselves and serve our brethren.

Let us meditate earnestly on the message conveyed by this parable.

Yours is the glory and honour, both now and forever. Amen.

Chapter 29

The Parable of the Lost Coin

"Or what woman, having ten silver coins, if she loses one coin, does not light a lamp, sweep the house, and search carefully until she finds it? And when she has found it, she calls her friends and neighbours together, saying, 'Rejoice with me, for I have found the piece which I lost!' Likewise, I say to you, there is joy in the presence of the angels of God over one sinner who repents." (Luke 15:8-10).

This parable, found in Chapter 15 of the Gospel of Saint Luke, is likened by one of the Early Church Fathers to an elegant musical interlude due to its harmony and arrangement. The entire chapter revolves around the theme of sinners and the rejected finding their redemption in Our Lord Jesus Christ, who surpasses all else and becomes their ultimate choice.

The joy in heaven resulting from a sinner's repentance is immeasurable. Angels rejoice at the return of even a single soul to God's embrace. This truth stands as the pinnacle of Our Lord Jesus Christ's teachings.

The chapter comprises three parables:

1. The Parable of the Lost Sheep: Here, the shepherd leaves

the ninety-nine to find one lost sheep, symbolizing God's pursuit of those who stray. The shepherd carries the sheep on his shoulders, both comforting and assisting it after its rugged journey.
2. The Parable of the Lost Coin: This parable is the focus of the current discussion.
3. The Parable of the Lost Son: This parable, the summit of all parables, will be explored in the following chapter.

This chapter commences with sinners and tax collectors drawn to Our Lord Jesus, eager to hear His words. In response, the Pharisees, and scribes grumble about Our Lord Jesus Christ's association with these individuals. Our Lord Jesus Christ's power of attraction stems from His unconditional love, compassion, acceptance, and healing for sinners. This magnetic force is a potent combination that drew the likes of Zacchaeus, the Samaritan woman, and others to Him. This attraction can be seen in some to this day, and blessed are those who are granted these Our Lord Jesus Christly attributes.

Those who feel self-righteous may resist sinners entering the Church, fearing the "corruption" of their children. However, Our Lord Jesus Christ's attitude toward sinners, demonstrated in the parables of the lost sheep and the lost coin, shows His deep concern for their well-being. Sinners find true solace and joy in Our Lord Jesus Christ alone. Their experience with Our Lord Jesus Christ transcends that of the self-righteous, for they possess the capacity to hear the Shepherd's voice, see Him, and feel His love.

Take Heed of Complacency: The Worm of Spiritual Life

Yet, there is a danger of slipping into complacency, as seen in the Pharisees who could not perceive Our Lord Jesus Christ's voice, sight, or love due to their busyness and self-righteousness. This serves as a reminder to introspect and evaluate our spiritual life. It urges us to question whether we allocate time for prayer, Bible reading, and listening to God's voice.

God's voice is often heard in the midst of quietude, not in the noise of life's distractions. Engaging in matters that do not concern us, and failing to recognize the need for God, leads to spiritual distance from Him. A lack of repentance distances the Lord from us.

The Parable of the Lost Coin is distinct from the Parable of the Lost Sheep, where the shepherd actively seeks the lost sheep and find him. Here we gain a sharper insight into God's grief over the loss of a sinner. The coin may not have great monetary value, but the woman turned her house upside down – almost desperately – to find it.

This parable also has a message for us who are servants: sometimes the church can lose people, but when she does, she ought to seek them out like this woman until she has found them again. The lighted lamp represents Our Lord Jesus Christ's incarnation, illuminating our search for the lost soul. When the person returns, we as the Church rejoice upon their return. The parable underscores God's deep longing for every soul, reflecting His sadness at their loss, diligence in searching for them, and ultimate joy upon their return.

The Early Church Father, Saint Gregory, likens the woman in the parable to God, the Heavenly Father, and His wisdom. The woman searches for the lost coin with a lamp, symbolizing the divine wisdom that searches for the lost soul. This coin bears the king's image, symbolizing humanity bearing God's image. When the coin is lost, the King's image is obscured. Similarly, sin separates us from God, and Our Lord Jesus Christ's incarnation allows us to see the path back to Him.

This parable calls every servant and congregant to light their lamps and diligently seek the lost coin. The Church's teachings and efforts aim to restore the lost image of the King within each soul that strays from God.

May we all possess the heart of Our Lord Jesus Christ, grieving for the lost and rejoicing over their return.

Yours is the glory and honour, now and forever. Amen.

Chapter 30

The Parable of the Lost Son

Then He said: "A certain man had two sons. And the younger of them said to his father, 'Father, give me the portion of goods that falls to me.' So he divided to them his livelihood. And not many days after, the younger son gathered all together, journeyed to a far country, and there wasted his possessions with prodigal living. But when he had spent all, there arose a severe famine in that land, and he began to be in want. Then he went and joined himself to a citizen of that country, and he sent him into his fields to feed swine. And he would gladly have filled his stomach with the pods that the swine ate, and no one gave him anything.

"But when he came to himself, he said, 'How many of my father's hired servants have bread enough and to spare, and I perish with hunger! I will arise and go to my father, and will say to him, "Father, I have sinned against heaven and before you, and I am no longer worthy to be called your son. Make me like one of your hired servants."'

"And he arose and came to his father. But when he was still a great way off, his father saw him and had compassion, and ran and fell on his neck and kissed him. And the son said to him, 'Father, I have sinned against heaven and in your sight, and am no longer worthy to be called your son.'

"But the father said to his servants, 'Bring out the best robe and put it on him, and put a ring on his hand and sandals on his feet. And bring the fatted calf here and kill it, and let us eat and be merry; for this my son was dead and is alive again; he was lost and is found.' And they began to be merry.

"Now his older son was in the field. And as he came and drew near to the house, he heard music and dancing. So he called one of the servants and asked what these things meant. And he said to him, 'Your brother has come, and because he has received him safe and sound, your father has killed the fatted calf.'

"But he was angry and would not go in. Therefore his father came out and pleaded with him. So he answered and said to his father, 'Lo, these many years I have been serving you; I never transgressed your commandment at any time; and yet you never gave me a young goat, that I might make merry with my friends. But as soon as this son of yours came, who has devoured your livelihood with harlots, you killed the fatted calf for him.'

"And he said to him, 'Son, you are always with me, and all that I have is yours. It was right that we should make merry and be glad, for your brother was dead and is alive again, and was lost and is found" (Luke 15:11-31).

This parable can be titled "The Father's Heart." The true protagonist of this parable is our Heavenly Father, whose profound love for humanity, especially sinners, knows no bounds. The events and teachings of Our Lord Jesus Christ within this parable transcend any human description. This parable of God's forgiveness calls us to "come to ourselves" as did the prodigal son, to see ourselves as being "in a far country" far from the Father's house, and to make the journey of return to God. We are given every assurance by our Master and Lord Jesus Christ that our heavenly Father will receive us with joy and gladness.

A Commentary by Saint Cyril of Alexandria

Let us start with a profound commentary by Saint Cyril of Alexandria (*Homilies on Luke*, Sermon 107) on this amazing uniquely crafted parable that represents the unlimited, unuttered, uncomprehended mercies of God!

I hear one of the holy prophets trying to win unto repentance those who are far from God, and saying, "Return, O Israel, to the Lord your God: for you have become weak in your iniquity. Take with you words, and return to the Lord our God." What sort of words then did he, under the influence of the Spirit, command them to take with them? Or were they not such as become those who wish to repent; such namely, as would appease God, Who is gentle, and loves mercy. For He even said by one of the holy prophets, "Return you returning children, and I will heal your breaches." And yet again by the voice of Ezekiel, "Return you altogether from your wickednesses, O house of Israel. Cast away from you all your iniquities which you have committed, that they be not to you for a punishment of iniquity. For I have no pleasure in the death of the sinner, as that he should turn from his evil way and live." And the same truth Christ here also teaches us, by this most beautifully composed parable, which I will now to the best of my ability endeavour to discuss, briefly gathering up its broad statements, and explaining and defending the ideas which it contains."

The narrative unfolds with the younger son's choice to separate from his father and embark on a journey of self-discovery, leading him to a distant land. This 'far country' symbolizes the destination those who intentionally distance themselves from God choose. Every individual, at some point, chooses to distance themselves from God. In this foreign land, they squander their inheritance and become spiritually impoverished, naked of God's righteousness and protection. *"He began to be in want."* This desolation often leads to feelings of need, of longing for warmth, love, and security -

needs only God can fulfil.

Let us take a moment to appreciate the remarkable courage and humility displayed by the prodigal son before we proceed with the parable's narrative. Despite recognizing the gravity of his actions and the pain he had caused his father, he refused to be paralyzed by shame. Instead, he made the courageous decision to embark on the journey back home, fully acknowledging the truth of his own decision and the subsequent wrongdoings. He was prepared to face any consequences, whether it be rejection, criticism, or awkwardness, upon confronting the father he had betrayed. Understanding the severity of his actions and their impact on others, he harboured no illusions about his situation and was resigned to the possibility of returning to the household as a mere servant, not as a beloved son. Nevertheless, undeterred by these prospects, he set out on the arduous journey home.

Many of us can readily recall instances in our lives when we have acted, spoken, or even thought in ways we are not proud of. These memories often stir discomfort within us because they confront our sense of pride and our very well-groomed self-image that we are very keen to portray. Regrettably, some individuals carry a heavy burden of shame throughout their lives—a burden largely stemming from their reluctance to humbly accept the truth about themselves.

The Reality of Sin and the Power of Repentance

Sin is inherently shameful as it signifies a rejection of our Lord and His divine intentions for us. On the contrary, repentance carries no shame because it signifies an embrace of our Lord and His divine intentions. It would have been tragic for the prodigal son to endure impoverished labour on a pig farm out of wounded pride, forsaking the opportunity for joyful reconciliation he found upon returning home. Similarly, regardless of our transgressions, thoughts, or words, regardless

The Parable of the Lost Son

of how far we have wandered from our Heavenly Father, the path of repentance offers redemption without shame.

The experience of being in need is a brutal realisation of one's limitations and vulnerability. In this state, the individual is often humiliated, their once-rich life reduced to servitude. They may find themselves among the swine, deprived of mercy, authority, and honour, a stark contrast to the abundant life they once enjoyed.

However, in this depth of degradation, a turning point occurs - *"he came to himself."* This phrase signifies the beginning of repentance. "Coming to oneself" involves a divine grace that awakens the soul to recognise its own poverty, death, and need for God. In the presence of Our Lord Jesus Christ's love and light, the soul can honestly acknowledge its state and seek refuge in the Father's embrace.

Repentance is not a passive process but an active one. Saying, *"I will arise now and go to my Father,"* initiates the encounter with divine grace. In response, the Father's love and compassion await, ready to welcome the repentant soul with open arms. Despite the soul's degradation, filth, and stench, the Father's love sees none of it. He rushes to embrace the returning child, demonstrating a love that transcends human comprehension. It is His love that brought this dead soul back to life: *"For my son was dead and is alive again."*

The prodigal son's return home was a resurrection from death to life, which is why his father called for such a great celebration. Lent prepares us to follow our Saviour to His Cross and the glory of the empty tomb at Pascha. We must die to sin so that we will be prepared to behold with joy our Lord's victory over death and to enter into eternal celebration of the Heavenly Banquet. There is no shame in preparing ourselves to accept such a great invitation. In fact, the only shame would be if we refused to accept it out of wounded pride.

The Unchanging Love of the Father

The father's reaction contrasts our human tendencies. He does not wait for the son's apology or explanation. Instead, he orders the best robe, a ring, and sandals for him, symbolising honour, authority, and restoration. The fatted calf is slaughtered, marking a celebration of the son's return. The father's proclamation, *"For my son was dead and is alive again; he was lost and is found,"* encapsulates the joy and love that fill this chapter.

This parable unveils God's heart towards sinners. Even when we were lost, alienated, and spiritually dead, God's love remains unchanged and open to us. Saint Paul's exhortation in Ephesians captures the immense dimensions of Our Lord Jesus Christ's love, which surpass human understanding: *"May be able to comprehend with all the saints what is the width and length and depth and height— to know the love of Our Lord Jesus Christ which passes knowledge"* (Ephesians 3:18).

I will conclude with an account I heard from a young man when we first arrived in Australia. After he arrived, his life was tied and marked by sin and spiritual emptiness for many years. He was working at a hotel restaurant on a terribly busy Christmas Eve. The heat of the kitchen made him feel light-headed, and the head chef suggested he step outside for some fresh air. As he recovered, his thoughts started to turn inward, and he reflected on his life and how unhappy and miserable he was. He came to himself, realise how far he had travelled, and prayed asking, "Lord if you will accept me back, please send me one of your serving priests to guide me and receive my confession" He had I have never visited a church since arriving in Australia, so there was no one in the Church who would have known him to reach out. But he had not even finished praying before he saw a flicker of black walk right past him. He called out to the priest and ran to catch up. The next day he was in church, and the sermon was on this very parable about the lost son. The priest saw this young repenting man crying

The Parable of the Lost Son

in the back of the church, and he then received the Sacrament of Confession, and his life came around 180 degrees back to God. See how swiftly God answered this man's prayer. How eagerly the Father's anticipates the repentant soul's return, bringing immense joy to heaven.

Truly, this parable centres on the Father's heart, His inexhaustible love for humanity, and His rejoicing over even a single soul's return to Him.

Yours is the glory and honour, both now and forever. Amen.

Final words

As we reach the conclusion of our exploration into the parables of the kingdom of God, it is essential to reflect on the profound journey we have undertaken together. Throughout these pages, we have delved into the depths of timeless wisdom and unearthed insights that resonate across the ages. What began as a collection of what seems to be simple stories, has transformed into a profound roadmap for navigating life's complexities with faith and grace.

These parables are not mere anecdotes from a distant past; they are living, breathing narratives that speak directly to the human condition. They offer us glimpses into the divine mystery and invite us to contemplate the deeper truths of existence. As we close this chapter of our journey, let us carry with us the echoes of these stories, allowing them to reverberate in our hearts and minds long after we have turned the final page.

In our modern world, filled with uncertainty and turmoil, the lessons of the kingdom of God are more relevant than ever. They remind us of the enduring power of love, the importance of forgiveness, and the transformative potential of faith. As we bid farewell to these parables, let us not simply close the book but rather carry its teachings with us as we navigate the complexities of our lives.

Let us go forth from this journey with renewed purpose and conviction, ready to embody the principles of the kingdom in all that we do. May we be beacons of light in a world shrouded in darkness, spreading hope, compassion, and understanding wherever we go. And may the lessons we have learned here guide us ever closer to the heart of God's eternal kingdom.

Final words

As we part ways, let us remember that the journey does not end here. The kingdom of God is not a distant destination but a living reality within each of us. May we continue to seek it, to strive for it, and to bring it forth in our lives and in the world around us. And may the grace of God accompany us on every step of the journey.

With gratitude for the wisdom, we have gained and hope for the journey ahead, let us embrace the closing of this chapter and the beginning of the next, knowing that the kingdom of God is ever-present, waiting to be discovered anew in each moment of our lives.

www.ingramcontent.com/pod-product-compliance
Lightning Source LLC
Chambersburg PA
CBHW031145160426
43193CB00008B/256